FRANK PEARCE ... ...
Plymouth. Soon af... ...
War II he voluntee... ... ...
Navy for Hostilities Only, serving as a gunner in defensively equipped merchant ships on the Atlantic convoy routes.

He joined the new cruiser HMS *Trinidad* at Devonport in 1941 when she was in the final stages of completion and served in her as Commander's Writer until her destruction in the Arctic when she was first torpedoed and later dive-bombed and sunk while escorting the Russian convoys.

In the years following the war, he became a schoolmaster at Thurlestone College, Dartmouth and later went into business as a hotelier. His retirement led to two absorbing hobbies, writing and oil painting. It was his interest in writing and his experience in the Royal Navy that led him to devote his time to the study of naval history.

RUNNING THE GAUNTLET

The Battles for the Barents Sea

FRANK PEARCE

FONTANA/Collins

First published in 1989 by Fontana Paperbacks
8 Grafton Street, London W1X 3LA

Copyright © Frank Pearce, 1989

Maps by Leslie Robinson

Printed and bound in Great Britain by
William Collins Sons & Co. Ltd, Glasgow

*This book is dedicated to
those who survived the Russian convoys
in World War II
And to the memory of those
who did not*

The crux of the problem is to make
the Barents Sea as dangerous for German
warships as they make it for ours.

Winston Churchill, 1942

CONTENTS

LIST OF PHOTOGRAPHS

LIST OF MAPS AND DIAGRAMS

ACKNOWLEDGEMENTS

The author acknowledges with gratitude the contributions provided by those who served in the ships mentioned in my book and to others closely associated with the events, among whom are:

Vice-Admiral Sir Arthur Fitzroy-Talbot, KBE, CB, DSO and Bar, RN (Retd)
Vice-Admiral Sir George Raper, KCB, CB, RN (Retd)
Rear-Admiral G. H. Collett, CB, DSC, RN (Retd)
Captain L. S. Saunders, DSO, RN (Retd)
Captain H. R. Harold, OBE, RN (Retd)
Captain J. W. Daniels, RM (Retd)
Captain G. Roberts, CBE, RD (Redt)
Lieutenant-Colonel R. F. V. Griffiths, OBE, RM (Retd)
Commander P. Rees, RN (Retd)
Commander J. Johnson, RN (Retd)
Commander A. J. Bailey, OBE, RN (Retd)
Commander J. B. Herapath, DSC, RN (Retd)
Commander P. R. House, OBE, RN (Retd)
Commander G. Mann, RN (Retd)
Commander F. Bradley, DSC, RN (Retd)
Lieutenant-Commander C. Broadway, RN (Retd)
Paymaster Lieutenant-Commander B. C. McLean, RN (Retd)
Flight Colonel Ernst August Roth, German Air Force (Retd)
Lieutenant-Commander K. V. Burnes, RN (Retd)

Edwin Dennerley   Arthur Start
Alan Devoud   Leonard Bradley

Michael Pascoe
William Fiddick
Harry Cook
Reginald Phillips
William Jones
Ronald Bennett
Charles Long
Frank Woodley

William Smitham
Fred Hodges
Reginald Levick
Peter Jefford
Jim Doyle
Jim Harper
George Stripe

Special thanks are due to Lieutenant-Commander J. R. Smith, RN (Retd), Chief Librarian at the Plymouth Naval History Library, for much assistance in research. Also to my son Derek for diagram contribution, to the staff of the Paignton Library and to Plymouth Sound radio station.

FOREWORD

The north Russian convoys have a place in the history of the Second World War high in the list of hard-fought battles. All convoy work requires determination and fortitude; inevitably the escorts are on the defensive, waiting for the attack, the enemy holds the initiative, and all too often the merchant ships are sitting ducks. It was the weather that distinguished the Kola Run from other convoy routes: in winter cold, dark and stormy but at least the hours for air attack were limited; in summer twenty-four hours of daylight allowed the bombers to come at any time – and they did.

Running the Gauntlet is indeed an appropriate title for this book because that is exactly what those convoys had to do. Passing close by the German bases in north Norway they were exposed to attack by aircraft, submarines and warships for the whole of their journey through the Barents Sea, their aggressors impelled by Hitler's determination that the supplies to Russia must be stopped at any price. By the summer of 1942 losses of both merchant ships and escorts had risen to an unacceptable level and Churchill proposed to Stalin that the convoys should be suspended, supplies being delivered by the longer but safer route round the Cape and through Persia. Stalin's reply was 'rough and surly' – as Churchill described it – virtually accusing the Royal Navy of cowardice, and it became a political necessity that the convoys should continue. The battles went on and eventually the tide turned in our favour, but at further cost.

Nearly fifty years have passed since the events that Frank Pearce so vividly describes in these pages. Those who went with the convoys to Russia are now old in years, but neither they nor their children have had to live through another world war. It is salutary to be reminded of the horrors of war if we learn the lesson that to live in peace, defences must be kept strong.

Lewin of Greenwich.

The Arctic Convoy Routes

Introduction

In the World War II conflict between the Allies and Germany, the strategic importance of the Barents Sea became paramount to both sides. In a bid to assist the Soviet Union, on whom the first and greatest impact of war fell so heavily, the British navy escorted vital convoys of Allied war materials through this wild sea area to northern Russia.

Thus was created the historic 2000-mile convoy route which became known as 'the Gateway to Hell'. In an attempt to stop these supplies reaching the hard-pressed Russian armies, Hitler established naval and air force bases along the coast of northern Norway from which he could launch his attacks. To fulfil the promise of aid to the Soviet Union, the Royal and Merchant Navies had to fight their way through the Barents Sea to the ports of Murmansk and Archangel against two forces – the merciless enemy and the almost impossible weather conditions.

The Barents Sea within the Arctic Circle covers 542,000 square miles, with average winter temperatures of −25°C. A tempestuous and dangerous water, in 1596 it brought disaster and tragedy to the famous Dutch navigator, Willem Barents, for whom it was named. Upon rounding the north of the archipelago of Novaya Zemlya his ship became trapped in ice, and Barents was compelled to winter there. He lived for only a week after he and his party managed to leave in open boats.

The battles of the Barents Sea convoys constitute one of the most poignant and dramatic episodes in British naval history. It was a time when heroism was commonplace, when hidden courage tempered fear and terror, and when survival depended on efficiency and speed.

This, then, is the story of the many convoys of the Barents Sea and the ships and men that sailed them, ships which, although outgunned and in action against impossible odds, fought with a gallantry worthy of the finest traditions of the Royal and merchant navies.

CHAPTER ONE

Lifeline to the Soviet Union

Across the top of the world, between Iceland and the eastern territories of the Soviet Union, stretches the Arctic Ocean, a vast expanse of tempestuous water covering some five million square miles. Within its limits lies the Barents Sea, bounded by Norway to the south, the Great Ice Barrier to the north, the huge island mass of Novaya Zemlya to the east and Spitzbergen to the west. It is notorious for being one of the most storm-tossed, merciless areas of water in the world, where endless gales bringing sleet, snow and hail whip up the water into a series of huge waves which hurl themselves in fury upon any ship in their path.

Before the outbreak of World War II in September 1939, most people had never heard of the Barents Sea, but between then and the end of hostilities in 1945 the attention of the warring nations was centred on this area of bloody conflict. Strategically it became the key factor in the Allies' defence against the resolve of the German chancellor, Adolf Hitler, to achieve world domination.

In June 1941, against the wishes of his two closest advisers, Admiral Raeder and Reichsmarschall Göring, Hitler launched a massive attack against the Soviet Union with 120 divisions under the code-name 'Barbarossa'. This offensive at first proved highly successful, and as the armies moved eastward, driving deeper and deeper into the heart of Russia, destroying factories and armament industries, that country's ability to maintain its defences became critical. For Great Britain Hitler's decision was a miracle of deliverance, for if instead he had turned his eyes westward and launched an invasion across the channel, Britain would have stood little chance. With only a few ill-equipped divisions, 95 tanks and fewer than 200 field guns, Britain was almost defenceless. Germany, on the other hand, was well equipped with 155 divisions, 10 Panzer divisions and 3000 armoured vehicles including at least 1000 heavy tanks.

The invasion of Russia provided the Allies with the precious gift of time — time to recover, time to rearm, time to prepare for the launch of a Second Front. The Germans had already subjugated most of Europe and, in a swift move to the north, had occupied Norway. Poised on the long coast-line from Cherbourg to Amsterdam, they were ideally positioned to launch an invasion; but the Führer, flushed with success but in a tangle of indecision, elected to strike first at his hated enemy, the Soviet Union.

The German drive through Russia was swift and devastating. Towns and cities fell quickly under the awesome weight of the advancing tanks and heavy guns. It seemed that the Soviet Union was doomed to destruction and it was clear to the British prime minister, Winston Churchill, and the American president, Franklin D. Roosevelt, that Britain's survival lay in providing the Soviet armies with every means of support. If Russia should fall, then Hitler would launch his delayed invasion of Britain. And the Russian leader, Marshal Joseph Stalin, left Churchill in no doubt about the 'critical situation confronting his people' and of their desperate need for weapons with which to repel the Nazi forces. Churchill, in reply, promised that everything that 'time, geography and our growing resources would allow' would be sent to help the Russians in their desperate situation.

The main source of this aid would, however, have to be the United States. In December 1940 the American president stated:

> There is absolutely no doubt in the mind of a very overwhelming number of Americans that the best immediate defence of the United States is the success of Great Britain defending itself, and that therefore, quite aside from our historic and current interest in the survival of Democracy in the world as a whole, it is equally important from a selfish point of view and of American defence that we should do everything possible to help the British Empire to defend itself;

and, later:

> We must produce arms and ships with every energy and resource we can command . . . we must be the great arsenal of Democracy.

Thus was founded the famous Lend-Lease Bill.

Later Lord Beaverbrook was sent to Moscow to conclude an agreement setting out the supplies which Great Britain and the United States could make available to Russia. The protocol ended with the words:

> Great Britain and the United States will give aid to the transportation of these materials to the Soviet Union and will help with the delivery.

Although Britain could ill afford to do so in the light of her own urgent defence needs, every effort was made to honour the agreement. As the prime minister said: 'We gave our treasures, and they were accepted by those who were fighting for their lives.'

The occupation of Iceland by American forces in 1941 proved to be one of the most successful strategic moves made by the Allies. It provided a base from which convoys carrying war materials for the Russian armies could operate, and in the autumn of 1941 the first of the so-called PQ series of convoys left Iceland for Russia. Convoys then left at ten-day intervals for either Archangel or the ice-free port of Murmansk in the Kola Peninsula.

In the early period of the war the most direct route was through the Arctic and Barents Seas. It was, however, also the most hazardous. The 2000-mile voyage from Iceland became increasingly dangerous as the Germans, determined to prevent supplies reaching Russia, began to establish submarine, destroyer and air force bases along the northern coast of Norway. From here they could control the whole of the Barents Sea. They attacked the convoys relentlessly, and although every effort was made by the Royal Navy to give escort protection to the merchant fleet, losses in ships and men were heavy. By November 1941, the German Central Army Group of von Bock was only thirty miles from the gates of Moscow.

The arrival of the first supplies of tanks, planes and guns from the Allies immediately raised morale among the Russian defenders. Resistance to the invaders increased, and the German advance was checked. Those ships that managed to fight their way through to the ice-free port and chief railhead of Murmansk were unloaded and their cargoes brought swiftly down the one and only railway track running south. Murmansk, formerly an insignificant fishing port, now assumed the utmost strategic importance for both sides, for it provided the means of transporting supplies from the convoys direct to the beleaguered cities of Moscow and Leningrad. While it is true that the greatest bulk of war material was eventually transported through the Gulf into Iran and thence into southern Russia, the weight of that operation did not really develop until after the end of 1943. Before that, during the period 1941–2 when the Soviet Union was on the point of collapse, the Arctic route provided the lifeline.

As Hitler and his chiefs of staff on the one hand, and Churchill and his war cabinet on the other, weighed up the situation, it was clear to both sides that the key to Russia's defence lay in the success or failure of the Arctic convoy route. Whoever controlled the Barents Sea at this time in no small part had the advantage in the bloody struggle between the two powers. Alive to the danger, Hitler reinforced his air squadrons in north Norway, even drawing on many of his most experienced dive-bomber pilots serving in the Mediterranean. Tactical plans were drawn up at Banak by Major Blodorn, operating the Stuka and Junker 88 dive-bomber squadron KG 30, and at Bardufoss by Colonel Ernst Roth, commanding the Air Torpedo Group of Heinkel 111 and 115 torpedo bombers.

In addition, long-range reconnaissance FW Condor aircraft were transferred to the six Norwegian bases.

These Condors were in fact the key to the German operation. They were able to fly long-range sweeps far out over the Barents Sea to find the convoys and guide the massed bomber squadrons to attack them. Their aim was to annihilate every ship that tried to get through.

Also in northern Norway, the three German naval ports of Petsamo, Kirkenes and Narvik were brought to 'battle-station' readiness with reinforcements of heavily armed destroyers of the Von Roeder, Leberecht and Narvik classes capable of speeds of 38 knots and over. Further south, ready to move out to attack convoy shipping when called upon, were heavy units of the German navy. These comprised the mighty battleship *Tirpitz*, the pocket battleships *Lutzow* and *Admiral Scheer*, the battlecruisers *Scharnhorst* and *Gneisenau*, the heavy cruisers *Seydlitz*, *Prinz Eugen* and *Admiral Hipper*, and the light cruisers *Leipzig*, *Köln* and *Emden*.

One of Hitler's most effective weapons, however, was the U-boat. Over fifty of these were operational from north Norway bases, roaming the entire area of the Barents Sea and Arctic Ocean. During the 1941–2 period alone, over sixty-three Allied ships were sunk with great loss of men and materials, a grievous blow to the Soviet war effort. On the British side, the urgent need for more ships in other theatres of war, the Atlantic and Mediterranean, was a constant problem for the First Sea Lord, Admiral Sir Dudley Pound. To even partially have met that need would have left the Arctic convoys at the mercy of air, surface and U-boat attack.

The most serious weakness of the British home fleet, however, and one which gravely affected the operation of the Arctic convoys, was the scarcity of aircraft-carriers equipped with efficient and modern planes. Without these it was virtually impossible to challenge Germany's air control of the Barents Sea. The shortage of anti-submarine escorts at this time was also grave, and all that could be spared to give some sort of protection were two destroyers, a minesweeper and two trawlers. Accompanying each convoy was one cruiser with perhaps another giving distant support from west of Bear Island. At the end of each convoy's 2000-mile voyage, as it neared the Murmansk coast, a few British mine-sweepers based at the Kola inlet would meet it to supplement the escort. Air support was almost non-existent. The little that could be provided came from Coastal Command based in Iceland, which covered only the first 150 miles; after that the convoy was on its own, vulnerable to whatever air attack the enemy wished to throw at them.

The escort protection given to the merchant ships was so inadequate as to be almost unbelievable, and the commander-in-chief of the home fleet, Admiral Sir John Tovey, constantly presented this fact to the Admiralty. But there was another factor of equal concern. Poised and ready to sail were heavy units of the German fleet. A strong force of British ships had to be kept at sea at all times to deal with them should they attempt to break out, and the only ships with equivalent gun-power and capable of dealing with the powerful German vessels were the battleships *King George V* and *Prince of Wales*. If the Germans succeeded in breaking through to the convoy routes they would not only paralyse the shipping lanes but would make almost impossible demands on the limited resources of the British fleet to find them and bring them to action in that vast area of sea north of the Arctic Circle.

Politically, relations between Stalin and Churchill were rather soured at this time by Stalin's demands that the Allies immediately launch a Second Front in Europe to relieve the pressure on his own armies, and he seemed quite impervious to any argument as to its impossibility. He also demanded that the size and frequency of convoys to Murmansk be increased. Often his uncomplimentary telegrams and unceasing demands reflected his sheer incomprehension of maritime warfare and lack of understanding of Britain's own perilous situation. Nevertheless, America and Britain ignored these criticisms and continued to honour their former agreement with Russia. In a letter dated 28 October 1941 to Sir Stafford Cripps, the British ambassador in Moscow, Churchill expressed his regret that Stalin should find it necessary to reproach Britain when in fact it had done all it could to help Russia at the cost of deranging its own plans for rearmament and exposing itself to the risk of a spring invasion. He reminded the ambassador that at the beginning of hostilities no one knew whether Russia would fight Germany or side with them, and that Britain was left unaided for a whole year while every communist in England was under orders from Moscow to attempt to hamper the war effort; he also pointed out that had Britain been invaded in 1940, Russia would have viewed the situation with indifference. The letter ended with the hope that Cripps would do his utmost to convince the Russians of the loyalty, integrity and courage of the British nation. Three weeks later, the Soviet ambassador in London visited Anthony Eden, the Foreign Secretary, with a message that it had not been Mr Stalin's wish to cause offence to the British prime minister, and that any adverse remarks that might have been made were with only practical and businesslike questions in view. Following this exchange, it appears that a more amicable relationship between the two leaders was eventually reached.

CHAPTER TWO

The Convoys

On 28 September 1941 the first of the codenamed PQ convoys, consisting of ten ships escorted by one cruiser, *Suffolk*, and two destroyers, left Iceland for Russia. Their cargoes were twenty heavy tanks and 193 fighter planes. By 6 November, the Russians had received 280 tanks and 500 aircraft.

But on 7 December there occurred an event which shook the world and must have sounded like the tolling of a death knell to Adolf Hitler. While peaceful negotiations were in progress between the Japanese ambassador in Washington and the American state secretary, Japan launched a devastating attack on the United States fleet in Pearl Harbor. Led by the commander of the Japanese Task Force, Vice-Admiral Nagumo, 400 fighter bombers and torpedo bombers attacked the harbour and destroyed five US battleships, seriously damaging another three. No declaration of war preceded this merciless attack on a neutral country. But while a jubilant Japan celebrated its so-called victory, the farseeing Nagumo commented: 'We have this day awakened a sleeping giant.'

Indeed this was so, for the United States now entered the war, throwing all her resources into the balance against the Axis powers of Germany, Italy and Japan. Her vast industrial output was turned over to the war effort on a massive scale, making large quantities of planes, tanks, guns and ammunition available for the Barents Sea convoys. It was up to Britain and Admiral Tovey to find enough suitable ships to give adequate protection to these new supplies.

During winter the Arctic ice barrier moves so far south as to leave a navigable stretch of water barely 200 miles wide between it and North Cape. Convoys were in fact sailing past the Germans' doorstep while at the same time struggling to overcome extraordinary navigational hazards. Freezing spray from huge waves formed layers of ice on the ships' decks so thick that smaller vessels were in danger of capsizing. And during the long winter darkness it was necessary to navigate without lights yet still retain convoy formation. It was a nightmare experience. Red-eyed lookouts peered through the sleet-laden darkness, fearful that they might crash into the ship in front or that the ship at the rear might collide with their stern.

Apart from damage caused by the battering of the storms, the first seven convoys managed to reach Murmansk without loss. Their success was due in part to the almost continuous Arctic darkness which made it impossible for enemy aircraft to locate their targets, but also to the time-lag in the build-up of German bases in northern Norway. But this good fortune was short-lived. On 10 January 1942 convoy PQ8 sailed from Iceland to Murmansk; it consisted of eight ships loaded with tanks and guns and was protected only by the cruiser HMS *Trinidad*, commanded by Captain Leslie Saunders, two destroyers, *Matabele* and *Somali*, and two minesweepers, *Speedwell* and *Harrier*. The completion of the new 8000-ton cruiser at Plymouth had come as a welcome relief to the home fleet after the demands made upon it from other theatres of war. She was a formidable fighting unit, carrying four triple 6-inch gun turrets, eight 4-inch anti-aircraft guns, in addition to many other smaller guns and six 21-inch torpedo tubes. She also carried two Walrus aircraft and was fitted with the latest in radar detection.

Slowly the convoy moved along on its voyage through the dark waters, its escorts continuously circling the perimeter, each ship fighting its own battle against the constant storms, ploughing into great seas, climbing the foaming crests or sliding crazily into the troughs with 35° readings on their roll indicators. In temperatures which could be as low as 40° below freezing, the crew would not dare place a bare hand on any metal surface for fear of leaving some of their skin behind. Eyelashes froze together and nostril hairs became little needles, so that a touch on the nose would bring the blood streaming. It is true to say that the Arctic climate in wartime cultivated a background of fear: fear of what would happen if the ship should be torpedoed and one had to take to the rafts, or worse, of how quickly death would come if it meant trying to swim for it. Here in the harsh desolate waste of the Barents Sea, framed by great ice masses and barely populated lands, the most buoyant spirits came to feel depressed and isolated from the normal life of the world. The pitiless cold, the savagery of the sea, the loneliness and the pervading presence of a brutal enemy all conspired to undermine the will to survive.

By noon on 17 January the convoy was nearing the approaches to the Kola inlet leading to Murmansk. Here the darkness seemed more intense. These were the most dangerous waters, where the U-boats gathered in force to intercept the incoming merchant ships. At 7.45 asdic contacts showed submarines to be in close proximity. (The 'asdic', named from the Allied Submarine Detection Investigation Committee, was an echo-sounding device which transmitted pulses under the surface that would bounce off a submerged object, such as a U-boat, giving its direction and approximate distance.) Just before 8.00 there was a violent explosion which lit up the night sky. The convoy's leading ship *Harmatris* had been torpedoed. The torpedoes, aimed at *Trinidad*, had missed the cruiser by only a few feet and sped on to hit the merchant ship. But while the crew were abandoning the vessel, the remainder of the convoy moved on, with the two destroyers *Matabele* and *Somali* dashing around at high speed dropping depth charges to deter the U-boat from making further attacks. In the meantime one of the U-boat pack moved on ahead of the convoy and waited. Three hours later, nearing the surface in the path of the ships, the U-boat dimly picked out the hulls of the approaching vessels and fired two torpedoes. It was these that found their target in the magazines of *Matabele*. Here, under the waterline, deep below the gun turrets, the steel-lined magazine chambers contained a store of explosive cordite and shells. A sheet of flame some 700 feet high shot into the night sky in an incandescent glare followed by a mushroom-shaped curtain of red-hot debris slowly falling back into the sea. The Royal Navy destroyer had disintegrated, hurling her crew of 200 into the ice-cold water. But another catastrophe followed. Several of the ship's own depth charges, which had already been primed and set to explode at various depths, now blew up beneath those who had not already been killed.

While *Somali* raced around the convoy trying to pick

up asdic contact, the minesweeper *Harrier* moved in to try to pick up survivors. The task was difficult and harrowing. The icy wind, bringing the temperature down to many degrees below freezing, produced an eerie effect with a thin swirling fog which froze like hoar frost. The decks were a mass of ice and the task of lowering the whaler with the falls frozen solid was tough and prolonged. Eventually the boat was lowered and the crew rowed towards the centre of the disaster area. As they approached they found the sea covered with a thick layer of fuel oil which had spilled out from the destroyer's tanks. Steering through a mass of debris they were just able to make out a number of men in their life-jackets floating upright, but closer examination showed them to be dead. As the crew rowed on they found the sea littered with men in this shocking and gruesome state, victims of the detonations and the freezing sea. Near the centre of the area they found the oil so thick they could hardly move the boat. The oars were simply dipping into a mass of thick sludge and getting them nowhere. Not far away they could hear men calling for help but it was now impossible to go further and they dared not show a light. From somewhere astern they could hear a faint chorus of shouts. With a supreme effort they went astern and within minutes found three men together and still alive. It was a formidable task to haul them aboard for they were far too weak to help themselves and in their slippery condition, enveloped in thick oil, it was difficult to find a hand-hold. At last it was done and they pulled back to *Harrier*, much to the relief of the ship's company because, as was said later, 'With the ship stopped we were sitting ducks.'

Once alongside there were similar difficulties in

embarking the survivors and this was only accomplished after scrambling nets had been lowered and heaving lines passed around the chests of the three men, who by this time were almost unconscious. All three had passed out by the time they were carried into the wardroom for medical examination. An hour later one was dead but the other two were responding to treatment and slowly recovered. They were the only two survivors out of a total of 200. It was a tragedy of the worst order and cause for intense depression for the crew of *Somali* at the loss of all their friends and their sister ship.

CHAPTER THREE

The Threat of the *Tirpitz*

The Battle for the Barents Sea had begun, and the Admiralty were in no doubt as to the bitterness of the conflict that would follow if control of the sea lanes were to be regained.

The port and railhead of Murmansk, built mainly of wood from the great timber forests covering the eastern Kola Peninsula, is situated at the head of the Kola inlet over 200 miles east of the North Cape of Norway. Its importance for the convoys lay in the fact that it remained ice-free all year round, and it was where most of the cargoes were unloaded. Although Archangel some 400 miles south-east could accept some of the supplies, its use was limited because for much of the year it was ice-bound. But Murmansk, with the German army's front line comprising General Dietl's 20th Mountain Army of 180,000 men barely twenty miles away, suffered severely from constant bombing raids launched by the German air force. Five miles from Murmansk on the eastern shore of the Kola River lies Vaenga Bay, a poor anchorage where British ships were obliged to anchor. Within the bay there was a pier and, near by, a hut in which survivors from bombed and torpedoed ships could be accommodated.

On 24 January 1942, having been at sea all night zig-zagging at high speed, the cruiser *Trinidad* arrived in

Vaenga Bay and moved in alongside the wooden pier to embark a pitiful company of human wreckage. They were 250 Poles who had spent the previous two years in Russia as prisoners of war after Stalin's invasion of their country at the outset of the war. As the officer of the watch received the Russian guard, names were read out and pathetic bundles of grey-green, topped with long unkempt hair, passed slowly up the gangway. Many had tears of joy running down their cheeks by the time they reached the top and some even fell upon the deck, kissing it again and again. Formed into small groups, they were distributed among the mess decks and made to feel at home. In broken English they were able to explain that most had worked in the salt mines in Siberia. Some showed their wrists and legs, raw from their chains. Some had been in solitary confinement for the last six months and in darkness except for half an hour every day when they were allowed the light of a candle. After the end of the war one of *Trinidad*'s crew working in Cardiff was approached by a man who appeared to recognize him. After a few preliminary remarks he introduced himself: 'I am Wilhelm Weber of Cracow. I was a prisoner of war aboard your ship HMS *Trinidad*. It is wonderful to see you again.' In the conversation that followed it appeared that most of the Poles had joined the Polish air force stationed at Northolt air base. In the air battles over France, Wilhelm Weber had been awarded the Polish equivalent of the Victoria Cross.

After the embarkation of the Polish prisoners on *Trinidad*, the cruiser took aboard a second cargo. Heavy boxes of apparently live ammunition were transferred on to the decks and quickly taken below to be stored in the bomb room safe in the bowels of the ship. A curious business really, for in fact the cruiser was well stocked with ammunition. Later, however, it was revealed that the boxes contained not ammunition but gold, several million pounds' worth of bullion in gold bars, payment for the war materials supplied by the United States and British governments, to be transferred to the United States treasury.

Unless one has fully experienced and perhaps been a survivor of the Arctic convoys, it is difficult to understand the deadly cold of the Polar oceans and to recognize what superhuman endurance was required of the crews. Escort vessels ploughing through the seas on the edge of the convoy shuddered under the impact of foaming mountainous waves that threatened to bury them. Torpedo tubes, guns and depth charges frozen solid with constant spray required endless attention to keep them operational for an all-too-possible emergency. Binoculars became useless as sleet and spray froze on the lenses. Wind-driven snow formed icicles on the faces of officers and men on duty watch. It was a time when the maximum of human endurance was called upon from every man. If and when a brief spell of sleep could be allowed, men did not sling their hammocks but slept fully clothed, propped up against a steam pipe to gain a little warmth. In these extreme conditions no man ever undressed, for the weighty garments he wore to keep out the cold would keep him afloat for a few minutes at least in the icy sea; if he was not plucked to safety in those few minutes he would die anyway.

There were, however, other factors undermining the will to endure. Not least of them was fear: fear of being trapped deep in the bowels of a sinking ship; terror that a bomb or torpedo might at any minute come tearing through the thin steel plating of the ship's hull to bring choking death in a hell of tangled metal. Added to this was exhaustion, brought about by little or no sleep. Constantly closed up at action stations, numbed by the bitter cold and tormented by seasickness, the strain took its toll. A cup of cocoa and a corned beef sandwich were infrequent luxuries. There were long nights of never-ending alarms caused by continual asdic contacts warning of the possible approach of enemy submarines. Fatigue over long hours groaned for a man to close his eyes for a few seconds, to let go, but he knew he dared not, that if he did he could endanger the ship and the crew. Although wrapped in thick duffel coats, jerseys and padded with layers of underclothes, men in exposed positions still shivered as they tried to protect themselves from the cruel wind and snow. Men wrapped themselves round rails and stanchions, against anything bolted down, to avoid being thrown across a steel deck or against sharp corners of the superstructure. The penalty of carelessness or forgetfulness was painful indeed.

It was in such conditions that on 1 March convoy PQ12 and the returning convoy QP8 sailed from Iceland and the Kola inlet respectively. In the meantime, intelligence reports received by the Admiralty from secret agents working in occupied Norway revealed that the battleship *Tirpitz* had been moved from the Baltic to Asafiord fifteen miles east of Trondheim, placing her in a favourable position to strike north at the convoy routes. This was confirmed by an Allied reconnaissance plane. The mighty battleship, pride of the German navy, constituted an enormous threat to the Allies. Of 43,000 tons, she carried eight 15-inch, twelve 6-inch and sixteen 4-inch guns, six aircraft and a complement of 2400 men, and could attain a top speed of 30 knots. To the British prime minister it was a matter of concern that *Tirpitz* should have moved to Trondheim. In a letter to the chiefs of staff dated January 1942 he wrote:

> The presence of *Tirpitz* at Trondheim has now been known for three days. The destruction or even the crippling of this ship is the greatest event at sea at the present time. No other target is comparable to it . . . If she were only crippled it would be difficult to take her back to Germany . . . The entire naval situation throughout the world would be altered, and the naval command in the Pacific would be regained . . . The whole strategy of the war turns at this period on this ship, which is holding four times the number of British capital ships paralysed, to say nothing of the two new American battleships retained in the Atlantic. I regard the matter as of the highest urgency and importance.

The news of the movement of *Tirpitz* gave Admiral Tovey probably even greater concern, for it was upon him that responsibility for the safety of the convoys rested. After considering every aspect of the situation he came to the conclusion that action by the German battleship to attack the next eastbound convoy was not only highly probable but imminent. In this he was correct. Unknown to him, the outward-bound convoy PQ12 had been sighted by a German reconnaissance plane and immediately reported to German command headquarters. Upon receipt of the news Admiral Raeder, commander-in-chief of the German navy, sought Hitler's permission to sail *Tirpitz* under the command of Vice-Admiral Ciliax to intercept and destroy the eastbound ships. With the destruction of *Tirpitz*'s sister ship *Bismark* by the British in May 1941 very much in mind, Hitler with some reluctance agreed. However, on 6 March, *Tirpitz* was sighted heading north with a destroyer escort at high speed by a British submarine on patrol north of Trondheim. To meet the threat Admiral Tovey, carrying his flag in the battleship *King George V*, placed his ships of the home fleet in a position to cover the convoy in the event of an attack. These were the capital ships *Renown* and *Duke of York*, the cruisers *Kenya* and *Berwick*, twelve destroyers and the aircraft-carrier *Victorious*.

If the two forces had met it would have been one of the great sea battles of the war, but it was not to be. In the poor visibility caused by snow squalls and patchy fog neither side detected the other, passing and repassing one another sometimes only a few miles apart. *Tirpitz* in her search for the convoy passed only sixty miles astern of the outgoing PQ12 and fifty miles ahead of the homeward-bound QP8 without seeing them and with no idea that Admiral Tovey's fleet was at sea in such concentration searching for her.

So the blind search went on until 8 March when Admiral Ciliax, with the mistaken impression that the convoy had probably returned to Iceland, headed *Tirpitz* south and homeward towards Trondheim. Admiral Tovey receiving intelligence reports of *Tirpitz*'s latest course, ordered the aircraft-carrier *Victorious* to fly off a striking force. At dawn on 9 March, in improving weather conditions, *Tirpitz* was sighted heading south at top speed west of the Lofoten Islands. A force of twelve torpedo-carrying aircraft attacked the battleship despite a formidable concentration of anti-aircraft fire. With great courage and determination they pressed home their attack. Twisting and turning to avoid the tracks of the torpedoes, *Tirpitz* escaped damage despite two torpedoes which hit yet failed to explode. It was a bitter disappointment to Admiral Tovey to have missed such an opportunity to achieve a success which would have had a lasting effect on naval operations all over the world. The opportunity was never to arise again.

CHAPTER FOUR

The Unlucky PQ13

On 21 March 1942 the cruiser *Trinidad* was again called upon to play her part in escorting a convoy through the Barents Sea to Murmansk. The circumstances were far different from her previous voyage, with PQ8, when constant darkness often denied the Germans the opportunity to attack. PQ13 comprised a merchant fleet of nineteen ships, deep-laden with tanks, lorries, aircraft and ammunition for the Russian armies. With improved daylight and visibility it was clear that the enemy would never allow these valuable cargoes to reach their destination without a supreme effort to stop them.

The escorting force, however, looked far too feeble to complete the task that lay ahead. In close escort were two destroyers, *Fury*, under Lieutenant-Commander C. H. Campbell, and *Eclipse* under Lieutenant-Commander E. Mack, and two small rescue trawlers, *Blackfly* and *Paynter*. Although Admiral Tovey had disposed the battleship *Duke of York*, the battlecruiser *Renown* and the carrier *Victorious* to provide distant cover several hundred miles away against a possible breakout of enemy ships, that knowledge would have given little comfort to the ships' companies even had they been told.

The convoy included ships of many nationalities and types. There were big ships and little ones, old and new, dignified cargo liners, tankers with their volatile loads, and rusty old tramps. All were vital, different in appearance but with a common purpose. Most carried deck cargoes, piled high and chained down to withstand the heavy seas that would sweep across them. There was freight of every description: food, iron ore, medical supplies, guns, bombs, planes, machinery, trucks and tanks. The few with nothing visible above decks would be ammunition ships; there would be no need for lifeboats if a torpedo found its way into one of these. The whole convoy had to travel at the speed of the slowest ship, the most modern being compelled to plod along with the oldest – a perfect target.

For the first four days the voyage was uneventful; things went well – almost too well. Then, on the 25th, one of the worst gales ever experienced in the Arctic war suddenly hit the convoy. It struck with such intensity that the storm became a greater threat than the enemy. The wind came out of the east like a raging giant, whipping the Barents Sea into a fury of tumultuous water. Each enormous wave, marble-flecked with foam, reared up in an awesome mountain of water sixty, seventy, eighty feet high, to break on the ships as though bent on engulfing them. It seemed impossible that any man-made structure could survive the impact of so great a mass of tumbling water. In the troughs between these great waves the quiet was unbelievable. Then followed the long haul, climbing slowly up to another wind-lashed crest, there to re-encounter the unbridled force of the tempest tearing at everything and screaming like a thousand devils. Periodically a giant among waves would break and come roaring down over the fo'c'sle, wrenching off anything that was not an integral part of the structure. Heavy boats, firmly secured in the davits and held in place by gripes, were snatched away like toys. Guard-rails were twisted and bent into grotesque shapes. Storage racks which supported rows of lifesaving Carley floats were rifled. Even a large reel that housed the steel hawser used for towing another ship, weighing a ton and a half and fastened securely to the deck, was picked up like a cotton reel and catapulted through the air into the boiling sea.

Freezing spray froze into ice as soon as it came into contact with the steel decks and superstructure of *Trinidad*, turning the cruiser into a power-driven iceberg. In the turrets, men who were thoroughly hardened to the normal heaving and lurching of a ship now became as seasick as any new recruit. Many had been closed up at action stations for what seemed like days on end. Utterly exhausted and numbed with cold, some dozed standing up while others draped themselves across gun barrels or whatever else would support them; all were in a state of mental inertia and physical exhaustion that made it difficult to summon up enough energy to carry out the simplest task.

Conditions below decks were chaotic. Anything that was not tied or screwed down found its way on to the deck to join the mass of gash that shifted with every movement of the ship. In the galley at the height of the storm, dinner plates, cups, saucers and cutlery all tumbled down in a deafening crash. Then, despite the protective fence around the stoves, still-simmering pots of hastily made soup spewed their gooey contents over everything. This happened when the cruiser took a monster wave beam on. Later the records showed that she had listed so far over that another two degrees would have capsized her.

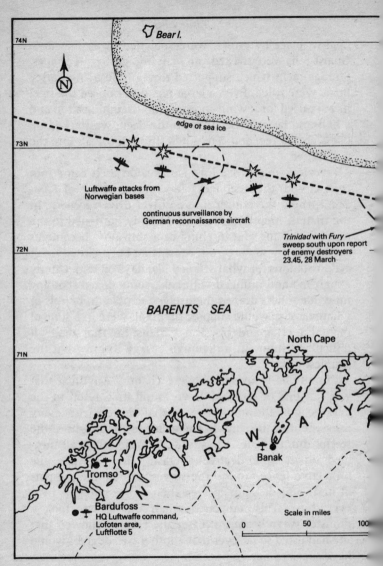

Convoy PQ 13: the battle area, 28 to 29 March 1942

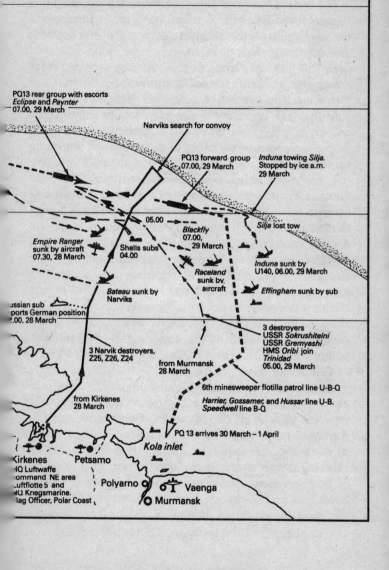

PQ13 rear group with escorts *Eclipse* and *Paynter* 07.00, 29 March

Narviks search for convoy

PQ13 forward group 07.00, 29 March

Induna towing *Silja*. Stopped by ice a.m. 29 March

05.00

Silja lost tow

Empire Ranger sunk by aircraft 07.30, 28 March

Shells subs 04.00

Blackfly 07.00, 29 March

Induna sunk by U140, 06.00, 29 March

Raceland sunk by aircraft

Effingham sunk by sub

Bateau sunk by Narviks

ussian sub reports German position 2.00, 28 March

3 Narvik destroyers, Z25, Z26, Z24

from Murmansk 28 March

3 destroyers USSR *Sokrushitelni* USSR *Gremyashi* HMS *Oribi* join *Trinidad* 05.00, 29 March

6th minesweeper flotilla patrol line U-B-Q

Harrier, Gossamer, and *Hussar* line U-B. *Speedwell* line B-Q

from Kirkenes 28 March

PQ 13 arrives 30 March – 1 April

Kola inlet

Kirkenes
HQ Luftwaffe
command NE area
Luftflotte 5 and
HQ Kriegsmarine.
Flag Officer, Polar Coast

Petsamo

Polyarno

Vaenga

Murmansk

Three days later the gale had eased but not before it had achieved what the German navy or air force could not accomplish – the complete dispersal of the convoy. The merchant ships of PQ13 were now alone, scattered over 150 miles of turbulent seas. For any convoy under attack the greatest chance of survival lies in its close formation and protective screen of escorts. But every ship in PQ13 was now a straggler, totally unprotected and an easy target for a U-boat. The destroyers *Fury* and *Eclipse* were some sixty miles to the westward, rounding up what vessels they could find, and slowly but surely the merchant ships were making contact with one another, forming groups of two or three and then joining up with other little groups. Over the hours that followed the destroyers shepherded the convoy into two separate flocks, one consisting of nine ships, five miles astern of *Trinidad*, the other some seventy miles ahead. Five of the stragglers found difficulty in rejoining any group. The *River Afton* found herself near Narvik, right on the enemy's doorstep, but eventually succeeded in reaching the Kola inlet. Another two, *Empire Ranger* and *Raceland*, steaming well ahead of the eastern group, were dive-bombed and sunk. Another, the *Bateau*, was also found and sunk by enemy destroyers.

On the morning of the 28th a German reconnaissance plane spotted the cruiser and convoy and immediately reported back to its headquarters. Two hours later the convoy was attacked by dive-bombers hurtling down through the low cloud to release their bombs before climbing steeply away. These attacks continued as relays of bombers from the coastal bases of Tromso, Banak, Bardufoss and Kirkenes flew in to support the raid. Despite the weight of bombs aimed at her, *Trinidad* escaped with only minor damage, thanks to the magnificent barrage of anti-aircraft fire put up by the gun crews and the adroitness of the avoiding action taken by the commanding officer Captain L. S. Saunders. By mid afternoon, after another merchant ship was sunk and two German planes shot down, the attacks had halted.

As if the bombing attacks and the battering from the storm were not enough, at midnight on the 28th came a signal from the Senior British Naval Officer, North Russia, informing *Trinidad* that a Russian submarine had reported three enemy destroyers heading towards the convoy from Kirkenes. These destroyers, having swept the area to the north-east without success, turned south-west, unaware in the heavy black snow clouds and intermittent fog banks that they were heading directly towards the convoy. At 08.45 that morning of the 29th, *Trinidad*'s radar plotted the approaching enemy at six miles; five minutes later it was a little over two miles. As the combined speed of the two ships gave a closing rate of 45 knots, it was clear that in a matter of minutes the crews of both sides would be looking down each other's gun barrels.

On the bridge and lookout positions all eyes strained to catch the first glimpse of the enemy through the snow-filled gloom. In the turrets the crews stood beside their guns, tense and pale, watching the faces of the telephone operators through whom would come the order from the transmitting station to open fire. Suddenly, with the unpredictability typical of the Arctic climate, the visibility cleared and there, immediately ahead at only one and a half miles, were three of Germany's big Narvik class destroyers each carrying guns equal in calibre and fire-power to the British cruiser.

These were units of the German 8th Destroyer Flotilla and later identified as Z24, Z25 and Z26. They were large vessels in comparison with British destroyers, having a complement of 320, a displacement of 2600 tons and a top speed of 38½ knots. They came in echelon formation, fountains of water creaming back from the slim bows as they stormed into battle.

At the same instant Captain Saunders gave the order to open fire, and everything that could be fired through a tube was fired: the main 6-inch guns, the 4-inch anti-aircraft, pom-poms and even machine-guns blazed out in a face-to-face confrontation. A curtain of fire crashed into the leading destroyer, Z26, immediately setting her on fire, and shells could be seen exploding amidships creating a mass of flame and smoke. The German ship, recovering from the ferocity of the assault, began to return fire, and two shells smashed into *Trinidad's* port side aft. Relentlessly the cruiser's salvoes crashed into and around the Z26. In desperation Commander George Ritter von Berger broke off the engagement and swung his ship to starboard, heading north-west into the nearest snowcloud.

With the leading German destroyer now out of action, director control was ordered to shift target to the second destroyer. Here again shells found their target with devastating accuracy, shattering her after guns. Nevertheless, at such close range *Trinidad* was in great danger from the torpedo-fire of these modern German destroyers. Anticipating this, Captain Saunders ordered the wheel hard to starboard. This meant that the ship now presented the minimum target to the enemy yet allowed *Trinidad's* after turrets to continue firing at the two destroyers. As the cruiser turned, two torpedo tracks were clearly seen as they passed harmlessly by to the port side. Two minutes later *Trinidad* again swung away to head due north at 26 knots to regain contact with the Z26. This time decreasing visibility caused the second and third ships to lose contact with their damaged leader. Fifteen minutes later *Trinidad*'s radar picked up the German two miles distant, and with speed increased to 30 knots she quickly overhauled the destroyer. Then, emerging out of the snow gloom, the shape of the enemy ship could be seen emitting clouds of billowing smoke.

At a little over a mile *Trinidad* opened fire with her forward A and B turrets, utterly destroying the enemy's after gun mountings. Desperately the Z26 zigzagged to escape further damage. Three more hits were registered just below the destroyer's bridge. *Trinidad* now swung to starboard to engage the enemy while passing obliquely across his stern. This manoeuvre had three tactical advantages: it permitted all *Trinidad*'s turrets to dominate the target; it prevented the German from using any of his eight 21-inch torpedo tubes from either side; and it reduced his opportunities of using his forward turret. As the chase continued *Trinidad* passed numbers of German sailors supported by their life-jackets in the sea, many already dead. They had either been blown overboard by the force of the explosions or had jumped to avoid being blown up and died from the effects of the ice-cold. It seemed incredible that Z26 could have taken so much punishment and still remain afloat. To finish her, *Trinidad* fired three torpedoes. Two of these, solidly frozen in their mountings, failed to leave the tubes, but the third travelled swiftly on its way towards the enemy.

But now there occurred one of the most bizarre incidents in British naval history. As the torpedo

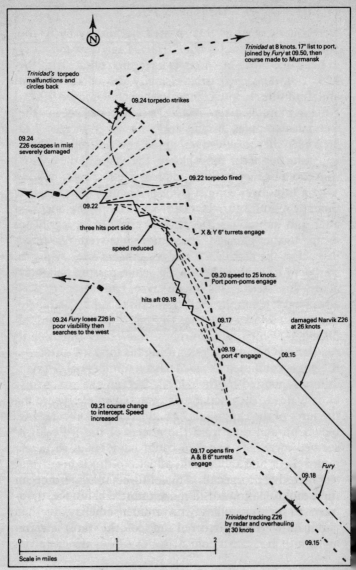

Trinidad at 8 knots. 17° list to port, joined by *Fury* at 09.50, then course made to Murmansk

Trinidad's torpedo malfunctions and circles back

09.24 torpedo strikes

09.24 Z26 escapes in mist severely damaged

09.22 torpedo fired

09.22

three hits port side

X & Y 6" turrets engage

speed reduced

09.20 speed to 25 knots. Port pom-poms engage

hits aft 09.18

09.24 *Fury* loses Z26 in poor visibility then searches to the west

09.17

damaged Narvik Z26 at 26 knots

09.19 port 4" engage

09.15

09.21 course change to intercept. Speed increased

09.17 opens fire A & B 6" turrets engage

Fury

09.18

Trinidad tracking Z26 by radar and overhauling at 30 knots

09.15

0   1   2

Scale in miles

The Torpedoing of *HMS Trinidad* 09.15-09.24, 29 March 1942

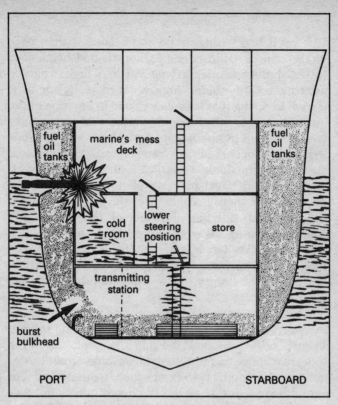

Position of Torpedo Impact, _HMS Trinidad_
(section viewed from stern)

continued to do so until, completing a half circle, it began to head back towards _Trinidad_. Incredibly, the gyro-mechanism controlling the rudder's behaviour had jammed from the effects of the ice-cold water and run amuck. It had the whole Arctic Ocean in which to run wild, yet it had swung round and headed straight back for the cruiser. Officers and lookouts stood helpless as the lethal silver missile carrying 750 lbs of high explosive raced in towards them. They watched in horror as it neared, knowing that it could explode in any one of the four magazines, which would mean that the cruiser would blow up in one mighty flash. But Captain Saunders, looking over the bridge parapet, casually remarked: 'You know, this looks remarkably like one of ours.' If ever the Royal Naval tradition of understatement was upheld it was then. Seconds later the torpedo plunged into the port side just forward of the bridge and exploded, tearing away the ship's side and leaving a gaping hole sixty feet by twenty. The chances of such a freak disaster were one in a million: it was the only time in British naval history that a ship ever torpedoed itself in battle.

The damage was calamitous, causing many casualties. The worst-affected area was in the transmitting station, set deep in the bottom of the ship. The explosion in the deck areas above had ruptured the oil tanks around them and seventeen of the twenty-one men in this department were drowned in fuel oil which poured into it. In other parts of the ship the explosion killed another fifteen. It left *Trinidad* critically damaged, virtually helpless and wallowing in the rising sea.

In the meantime one of the British destroyers, the accompanying *Eclipse*, picked up a radar contact at two miles and decided to investigate. It proved to be the mortally dmaged Z26. Soon they came to within 500 yards of the destroyer, and without further ado *Eclipse* opened fire with her one and only 4.7-inch forward gun. The enemy's speed had not been impaired and without attempting to return fire she tried to escape into the mist. If at that moment Z26 had still had her 5.9-inch after guns operational she could have blown *Eclipse* to pieces; but it could be clearly seen that her three after turrets were completely demolished as a result of *Trinidad*'s earlier shelling. One gun was cocked up into the air, another hung crazily over the side, while a third seemed to be locked on to the port beam position pointing down towards the sea.

Eclipse, hard on the heels of the Z26, took up the chase and soon began to overhaul. Commander Ritter von Berger made desperate efforts to bring his ship around and get his forward gun to bear but the commanding officer of the British destroyer, Lieutenant-Commander Mack, was more than a match for him and was not to be denied his victory. Skilfully anticipating every move, he clung tenaciously to the astern position as the German twisted and turned. He could not afford to make a single mistake because, given the chance, the more powerful forward gun of his adversary could quickly destroy his ship. Contact was almost lost on several occasions when severe snowstorms brought the visibility down to a few hundred yards, but fuel oil leakage from the stricken ship left a trail that could easily be followed.

Eclipse's gun was now finding its target and shell after shell slammed into the fleeing destroyer, though for the gun's crew conditions were almost impossible. As *Eclipse* raced on through the blizzard the ice-cold spray came pluming over the bow, falling in a freezing downpour on the forward gun mounting. Unlike their German counterparts, the British crews did not have the shelter and protection of a steel turret to encase them. They were out in the open, and any scrap of flesh left exposed would be flayed by ice particles. The gunlayers had to aim with smarting eyes peering through frozen eyelids as they strained to stay on target. Loading numbers had to force their numbed hands and frostbitten fingers to grasp the shells which first had to be kicked free of the shrouds of ice that bound them to the ready-use racks. *Eclipse* was now very low on fuel and this made her sensitive and liable to pitch and roll much more than usual. She listed excessively each time the wheel had to be put over to counter the enemy's avoiding action. The gun crew's feet on the ice-covered deck would then slide from under them, thus further hampering the passage of heavy ammunition into the ever-hungry breech.

German sailors could now be seen jumping overboard to avoid destruction by the exploding shells even though their death was more certain once they were in the water. As pitiful as their plight might seem, *Eclipse*'s crew remembered the scores of merchant seamen that had gone the same way in earlier convoys, and the many more that would do so until the enemy was defeated. Then there were the 200 men of the *Matabele* who had recently been killed in these same frozen waters as a result of a U-boat attack.

Mack had no alternative but to make certain that Z26 was eliminated. One shell from *Eclipse*, hitting the enemy aft, must have penetrated one of the cordite magazines for there was a powerful explosion, though this did not reduce his speed. Minutes later he suffered another direct hit on the starboard side and this shell must have exploded in the boiler room for at last the vessel slowed down and finally stopped. *Eclipse* cautiously approached. The stern of Z26 was now awash, with the after turrets and decks a complete shambles.

Gradually the British ship moved up along the starboard side. The oerlikon and machine-gun crews watched tensely for the slightest sign of retaliation. But the big destroyer was like a ghost ship, with no sign of life and slowly sinking. Mack swung the bows of his ship across the enemy's and came down her port side giving the order 'torpedo ready'. Suddenly, without warning, two shells came screaming out of the sky, one falling just astern and the other some 200 yards ahead. For the second time that day, fate had turned the tables.

Undetected, the two sister ships of Z26 were approaching at speed through the snowclouds, firing with their main armament as they came. Unfortunately the snowstorms were abating and visibility improving. Deciding that the situation and conditions were far from suitable for him to try to take on the two big ships, Mack made off at top speed. He left the remaining torpedo unfired in case there was a chance of using it on his two new opponents. With shells falling all around, and zigzagging wildly, *Eclipse*'s after gun was able to score a direct hit on one of the pursuing vessels, but she herself received two direct hits which, exploding aft, ignited some cordite charges causing heavy casualties among the ammunition parties. It was not until twenty minutes later that she reached the comparative shelter and safety of the nearest snowcloud. Below and above decks the situation was bad but not critical. Shells had holed her sides extensively and carried away aerials and part of the funnel. One rating had been killed and a dozen seriously wounded. Most of the crew were by now in a state of exhaustion after the long hours spent closed up at action stations, and double tots of rum were handed out. *Eclipse* had had enough for one day.

But just at that moment the snowstorm lifted and there, clearly visible on the port bow less than 400 yards away, was a large U-boat on the surface. Even as the two enemies recognized each other Mack saw the wakes of two torpedoes converging on him. With helm hard over, alarm bells ringing and action stations sounding again, *Eclipse* managed to swing away in time to allow the two deadly steel fish to pass harmlessly by and disappear astern. Speeding round to port to commence a run-in for a depth charge attack, Mack could see the U-boat beginning a crash-dive. With *Eclipse* working up to full speed and the U-boat so close he had very little time to make decisions and even less time to execute them. Every second counted if he was to catch the U-boat near enough to the surface to ram her and give his gun crews an opportunity to score a hit before she disappeared.

But time was not on the side of the destroyer. The U-boat was fast disappearing, and when *Eclipse* arrived at the spot where the submarine went down the only signs of its existence were the swirls and eddies caused by a hasty crash-dive. Way below the surface the enemy was escaping, and although *Eclipse* dropped pattern after pattern of depth charges there was nothing to indicate they had caused any damage. With fuel stocks now dangerously low and his crew's endurance taxed to breaking point, Mack abandoned the hunt and headed for the Kola inlet and Murmansk.

To return for a moment to the Z26. Out of the German destroyer's complement of 320 men, 246 were killed in the engagement. Among the survivors was the commanding officer Captain George Ritter von Berger, who was to be killed towards the end of the war. Many years later his widow wrote to the present author giving her husband's account of the engagement:

> As Z26 was sinking, the Captain although badly wounded in the face and legs managed to drag himself off the bridge and arriving at the rail gave the order to abandon ship. The men gave three cheers and jumped over the side into the icy water. As he floated away he was sure he would never be picked up alive but a life-boat from Z24 arrived almost at once and he was carried aboard unconscious. Months later, having recovered from his wounds, he was appointed leader of the destroyer flotilla at Narvik in Z32. When the Allied invasion of Normandy took place, his ship was sunk in the channel, and captured by the French, he was imprisoned in the fortress of Gironde Sud.

She then gives an account of her husband's death:

> In the night, my husband being a prisoner alone in a house guarded by ragged soldiers was brought to a lonely place and killed by machine guns. He was found some days later and buried in a cemetery at Berbuil, Charente-Maritime, near Saintes.

While *Eclipse* had been engaged with the German U-boat, in *Trinidad* optimism had been rising with every hour. Down below, the damage-control parties were performing something only short of a miracle. The fires in the Royal Marines' section had gradually been brought under control and the small-arms magazine immediately below this mess deck had been successfully flooded to remove the danger of it blowing up from the heat generated above. Just as this operation was reaching its final stages a second fire broke out in another mess deck caused by hammocks and clothing igniting. The blaze was intensified by oil which gave rise to volumes of black smoke. Above, the sick bay was so gravely affected that water had to be played on the deck to keep it cool.

As several attempts to extinguish the fire on this mess deck proved unsuccessful the area was sealed off and the fire allowed to burn itself out. By a concentrated effort of pumping and counter-flooding, the cruiser was gradually decreasing her list. Even so, it was no time for rejoicing for she was still lying well over, deep in the water, lurching with every sea, quite helpless and a perfect target for any enemy U-boat or surface vessel which might chance to see her. The surviving boiler room was hard put to provide enough steam to keep steerage way on the ship. Her speed was only 4 knots, barely enough to set course for Russia some 150 miles to the south-east.

Meanwhile, U-boats had been converging on the approaches to the Kola inlet with the intention of intercepting any shipping making for the safety of the Russian port. Early that afternoon, out on the port bow, the destroyer *Fury* sighted a surfaced submarine about 500 yards distant. The report from *Eclipse* that they had just failed to sink a U-boat only increased Lieutenant-Commander Campbell's determination to take every advantage of this opportunity. Swinging *Fury* round in a tight circle that made her heel over until her gunwales were almost awash, Campbell bore down on the submarine at top speed in an attempt to ram her. The U-boat captain had been taken unawares by the sudden appearance of the British ship through a rift in the snowcloud and now, with disaster almost upon him, he frantically crash-dived his boat before the sharp bows of the oncoming destroyer cut him in two. *Fury* was over the spot in seconds, but it was too late. The U-boat was now deep below the black waters, twisting and turning to avoid the depth charges which would inevitably fall on or near it.

In *Fury*'s asdic compartment the operator had already established a fix on the quarry. The constant pinging echo confirmed a strong contact, and minutes later the first of the powerful depth charges shot from the destroyer's decks. Astern of *Fury* the sea boiled and erupted as the charges exploded. Seconds later the echo-sounder indicated that the enemy was still there, still active and constantly changing direction.

And so the deadly game of cat-and-mouse went on, with *Fury* darting this way and that in the tortuous trail of the submarine. For the next fifteen minutes patterns of depth charges catapulted from the destroyer's decks, raising huge fountains of water above the sea. Suddenly there came a dull underwater explosion and up from the depths burst a great gout of oily water followed by a mass of debris that thickened and spread in an ever-widening pool of discolouration.

The chase was over; *Fury* had had its first U-boat. Later the submarine was identified as U585, of 1700 tons and with a complement of fifty-seven crew. This success, coupled with another scored by the destroyer *Sharp-shooter*, which sank a U-boat in defence of the returning QP9 convoy, was encouraging since up till then no U-boats had been sunk on the Russian convoys.

While *Fury* had been pursuing U585, merchant ships in the main body of *Trinidad*'s convoy were struggling onwards as best they could, though they were in no condition to keep close station. Some were suffering from the effects of near misses in the earlier attacks, others were listing because their cargoes had shifted in the great storm, and the badly damaged *Harpalion* was following a long way astern. The crews of these merchant vessels had already performed a magnificent job in bringing their ships as far as this, but they still had one more obstacle to overcome before they would be able to rest in the shelter of a protected harbour. Somehow they had to get past the ambush the U-boats had set. The *Effingham*, a few miles ahead of the forward group, took the first torpedo which, exploding in her boiler room, sank the vessel in minutes. Even though some of her crew were able to reach a lifeboat, only a few survived the weather conditions.

Trinidad, though protected, was still in difficulties, for with the fading light the weather worsened. The north wind rolled up nasty seas upon her port quarter causing her to yaw from port to starboard. Within an hour it was dark, and even if the U-boats could hear the cruiser they could not see her. By midnight, such was the fickle nature of the climate, the wind had dropped, the clouds dispersed and a quiet calm came over the unruly seas. But at the same time out came the moon, a large, full, round moon which lit up the ocean far better than the sun had done on the previous day. Apprehension among the crew rose with every passing hour, knowing that *Trinidad*'s black silhouette against the silver sea would be clearly framed in the periscopes of the waiting submarines.

It was then that the engines stopped. For some time salt water had been finding its way into the pure water used to feed the boilers. Once this salt reached danger level the boilers had to be shut down to prevent serious damage. The cruiser drifted to a standstill. The engine room staff, fully alive to the danger of the situation, worked like demons to clear the trouble. A most eerie silence followed the shutting down of the ventilation fans. Like a bad dream, there was an air of unreality hanging over the scene. Men stood around on the upper deck and talked in whispers, each aware of a spine-chilling tension, watching the silver sea rippling in the moonlight.

At first there was only one sound to be heard, the gentle lapping of water against the ship's side, but later, as the repairs developed down below, the clang of hammering reawoke fears of discovery. Surely every U-boat for miles around would hear the noise. But their luck held. As a sitting duck they were spared the destruction which seemed inevitable. In the distance the escorts worked like gun-dogs searching for game, repeatedly circling and backtracking to keep the U-boats under. Every second seemed like a minute and each hour an eternity. Just aft of the hangar deck an old timer with grey hair, certain that this would be the end, sat calmly, whittling down a piece of wood to form a bung to fit into the hole of an empty oil drum in the hope it would keep him afloat until he was picked up. He chose to ignore what he must well have known, that the temperature of the sea was his most deadly foe.

At last the repairs were finished and the propellor shafts began to turn. *Trinidad* was on her way again and the ship was alive and full of hope once more, and with the light of dawn came the Kola inlet only twelve miles away. Two hours later there were only five miles to go and by noon, finally and with great thankfulness, *Trinidad* arrived to anchor opposite Rosta.

It was not until 1 April that the last of the merchant ships arrived, making fourteen in all to complete the voyage. Over a quarter of PQ13 had been lost by enemy action. *Trinidad* had been severely damaged and temporarily put out of action by her own torpedo, and *Eclipse* was badly mauled by gunfire. Against this the Germans had lost their large modern destroyer Z26, and another had been damaged. In addition U585 had been attacked and sunk. The concentration of German destroyers, submarines and bombers on PQ13 clearly demonstrated the importance they attached to cutting the supply route to Russia. PQ13 was the first convoy to be subjected to such an onslaught, but both merchant ships and escorts had the right to be proud of the parts they had played in bringing the convoy through.

The crippling of *Trinidad* was, however, a serious setback. No one was more aware of this than the First Sea Lord, Admiral of the Fleet Sir Dudley Pound. Such misfortune had happened in the face of mounting German opposition and lengthening hours of daylight when more protection was needed. The change from the almost perpetual darkness of winter to the constant daylight of spring required a review of the conditions under which convoys were to sail. As the days lengthened it became easier for German reconnaissance planes to locate them, and this, combined with the build-up of enemy surface ships, submarines and aircraft in northern Norway, indicated that an increase in the number and weight of attacks was to be expected. It was therefore imperative for *Trinidad* to be repaired as quickly as possible to resume her escort duties.

After some protracted and entirely unnecessary negotiations, the Russians, through the Senior British Naval

Officer in Murmansk, finally gave permission for the damaged cruiser to move into the only dry dock at Rosta. They seemed singularly unhelpful, only allowing the use of the dock on the understanding that the docking would be carried out by the ship's crew. Incessant bombing of the dockyard had put the electric power out of action, so the ship had to be pulled into the dock manually. Once there, massive tree trunks had to be cut to size to shore the ship in place between the dock walls. As the water was gradually pumped out of the dock, the full extent of the damage could be seen. Apart from the huge gaping hole, three decks were laid bare and many bulkheads had completely disintegrated. Opposite the main hole, another on the starboard side gaped wipe open. Steel plates were needed to repair the ruptured hull, but requests made to the Russians for plates were in vain: 'Yes, there are steel plates somewhere in the dockyard but no one knows where. In any case, they are buried under tons of snow and impossible to find.'

In the event an urgent signal was sent to the Admiralty for suitable plates to be sent up on the next convoy. And there the matter had to be left until their arrival in mid April.

CHAPTER FIVE

The Merchant Ship *Induna*

And what of the scattered merchant ships? Although most had managed to converge and join the two main groups, three vessels found themselves well to the north and were soon subjected to bombing attacks by Junker 88 dive-bombers. They were the *Induna*, the *Silja* and the *Ballot*. Although they did not receive direct hits, much damage was caused by near misses. After the attacks had ceased the little trio tried to find refuge from the U-boats by steering a course inside the ice barrier — so far inside, however, that they became stuck in the ice field and late that night somehow lost track of one another. Later they managed to free themselves and set a course for Murmansk.

Free of the ice field, they were still close enough to it to assume that U-boats would not operate so far north, and optimism rose among *Induna*'s crew with every hour that passed. There was also the comforting possibility that ships of the following convoy might meet up with them. At their present speed, another twenty-four hours would see them anchored safely in Vaenga Bay. The wind had risen to near gale force, producing a rough sea, another factor which could lessen the likelihood of enemy action.

No one saw the tell-tale silvery wake of the periscope that moved in on their starboard beam. The U-boat commander must have viewed the scene with incredulity. A careful survey round the horizon showed no other ship in sight; it was all too simple. Not even the lookouts saw the track of the torpedo on its way to plunge into the starboard side well aft. This ignited the cargo of gasoline and the resulting explosion threw everyone off their feet. Flames shot up to a tremendous height and in seconds all the after part of the ship was a blazing inferno. The two Bofors gunners, who had just come on duty on the poop deck, ran, jumping through the flames until they were clear. But the remainder were still in their accommodation on the deck below and perished instantly.

Minutes after the alarm had sounded the starboard lifeboat was lowered. By the time the second officer, Mr Rowlands, had destroyed the confidential papers and reached the boat it was full. Indeed it was over-full. Although its maximum capacity was twenty-five, the boat now held thirty-three. The port lifeboat, which had been lowered safely into the water, was proving hard to keep alongside. The men who had already climbed into the boat were being choked by smoke from the fire. The chief officer from the deck therefore ordered them to go round the stern to the starboard side and take off the remainder. As they were pulling away, the black dripping hull of the U-boat surfaced only 100 yards from the starboard lifeboat. It was a large craft about 250 feet long. She had a jumping wire and was armed with a small 20 mm gun just forward of the conning tower. The number '140' was clearly visible.

The men in the boats watched her apprehensively, for they had heard stories of U-boat crews machine-gunning survivors in boats. But there were also stories of U-boats distributing provisions and blankets and bidding survivors 'Good luck' when they left them. Which would it be on this occasion?

The submarine edged in towards the burning ship, firing a second torpedo which exploded in no. 4 hold with a tremendous blast, lifting the ship and discharging a mass of debris into the air. As the men in the boats waited, the stern of *Induna* settled rapidly and the bows began to rise high out of the water. They watched in horror as the remaining officers and crew struggled to launch the small jolly boat. In a roar of escaping steam, internal explosions and the sound of inrushing water, the bows rose higher until they were almost vertical. Then, stern first, she plunged straight down, taking the men left on deck with her. From the time the first torpedo had struck to her final disappearance had been just thirty minutes.

For a while the U-boat stood off, then she submerged and was lost from view. In the turbulent seas the two boats now lost contact with one another. In the crowded starboard lifeboat the men scanned the heaving sea for their comrades in the other boat, but all that could be seen was an endless waste of tumbling seas. There was little time to hang about, and it was as much as the second officer could do to prevent the boat from falling into the troughs broadside on to the waves, even when the crew were rowing as hard as they could. Fortunately a force 6 wind was astern and blowing them in the direction of their destination – Russia.

A sober assessment of their situation gave Mr Rowlands little ground for optimism. They were about 175 miles from land, fully exposed to sub-zero temperatures in an open boat and subject to gales and snowstorms without warning. They were so overcrowded that not only would the men be unable to take exercise to keep warm but attempts to row would also be hampered. The boat was leaking badly and, with seas breaking over the side, it required constant baling with buckets to check the rising water level. To the men Mr Rowlands presented a cheerful picture of their chances: they had food and water, and the following wind, if assisted by sailing and rowing, would help them on towards the land. But in his own mind he had to admit it would be a race against time. How long could their bodies hold out against the wet and the cold before they froze?

The men seated on the thwarts were the most fortunate because the exercise of rowing kept the blood circulating. For the rest it was sheer hell. The injured lay on the bottom boards in freezing water. One of them was the donkeyman, who had been severely burned and was now in great pain, every jolt of the pitching boat adding to his torture. Others sat propped up against the sides or perched precariously in the bows, while the remainder managed to bunch themselves together in the stern sheets. Taking charge, Rowlands decided to hoist sail. Considerable time elapsed before they were able to step the mast and set the jib-sail, the trouble being that he was the only one who knew how to handle a boat as most of the men with him were from the boiler room.

In this manner the little band of survivors set out on their long haul to Russia on the morning of 30 March. Although the boat was running before the wind, the men rowed in spells to keep as warm as possible. But when night fell it grew much colder and hands became too numb to grasp the oars any longer. In the boat's lockers were seven bottles of whisky and these were passed round to combat the cold, with a warning to drink only sparingly. Unfortunately some of the men drank a great deal of the spirit and fell asleep – a few into too deep a sleep.

As the grey streaks of dawn appeared, those who had survived the night roused themselves to face the new day. It was soon discovered that not only had the donkeyman slipped mercifully out of this life but six of the older seamen who had drunk deeply the night before were lying stiff and frozen and would never wake again. With the chill awareness that any one of them could suffer the same fate in the hours ahead, the remaining men lifted the bodies of their shipmates over the side and watched them float away. No one dared to express the growing anxiety and gnawing fear arising in their own hearts.

All that day they sailed on, occasionally assisting their progress with ever-weakening attempts to hold and pull the oars. The insidious effects of frostbite were undermining their endeavours. None of them wore sea-boots, which meant that their feet and ankles were in water all the time. The foresail was unlashed and rigged as a shield against the wind and water on the weather side of the boat which was fully stored with milk tablets, biscuits, chocolate and the like. But food was not a real problem; what everyone craved was water to drink. The water in the containers was frozen into solid blocks, and the only way to get at it was to break open the containers and suck lumps that could be hacked off. Even the pemmican among the stored food was frozen into unmanageable masses.

That evening, with the sharp lesson of the previous night very much in their minds, the men took only a small sip of whisky before settling down for the night. In the ensuing misery and discomfort of the swirling snow and biting wind everyone felt the cold penetrating deeper and deeper. Early on the following morning, 1 April, Mr Rowlands' roll call revealed that two more had died during the night. It was only with the greatest difficulty that the bodies were lifted out and placed in the water.

As the day wore on the crew looked out over the turbulent sea with growing despair, wondering how much longer their bodies could withstand the exposure. From the original thirty-three numbers were now down to twenty-three. While the second officer steered the rest huddled together as best they could. In this way they could get some shelter from the wind and some warmth from each other. A few men's legs had become so numb they were unable to move without assistance. During the afternoon one of the greasers slumped over his oar and rolled to the bottom of the boat. An hour later a steward, one of four men in the bows, slid forward into a coma from which there would be no recovery. These two had to be left where they had fallen, as by now no one had the strength to lift the bodies over the side.

At dawn of the fourth day any hopes of seeing a coastline were dashed by the sight of the unbroken monotony of a heaving sea. Four more men had lost their fight for survival during the night and only seventeen remained alive. As the hours of daylight passed and early evening approached with the prospect of another cold remorseless night, the last few shreds of hope were turning into utter despair. Only the hardiest men with the staunchest of spirits could have lasted this long; were even they to be defeated?

Just before six, with evening almost upon them, one

of the crew in the stern saw a speck on the horizon and mumbled something about a ship. All eyes scanned the dim ridge of sea in the fading light and Mr Rowlands, his binoculars shaking in his hands, studied the object with all the presence of mind he could muster. The rest watched him with quickening pulses. The speck was certainly not a ship, but it was impossible to identify at first for it was at least five miles away. Suddenly it dawned on Mr Rowlands. Hardly trusting himself to speak, he turned to the others and said, 'Lads, it's a lighthouse – we've made it.'

In fact it was Cape Sviatoi lighthouse on the eastern coast of the Kola inlet. Even in their extreme weakness they managed to reach out and clasp one another's hands. Too exhausted to cheer, the men wept openly. They were going to be alright. Within minutes came the sound of approaching planes. Soon three Russian fighters were clearly visible and they flew around the boat several times. After acknowledging the flag which the crew held up, the fighters flew back to the coast to bring help. At eight o'clock, just two hours later, a Russian minesweeper came alongside to take them aboard. Their numbed and swollen legs had no power to stand. Their earlier exhilaration had drained the little strength remaining and left them frozen effigies of living beings. In this helpless state they could not get themselves out of the boat, so the Russians had to come aboard to fasten ropes to hoist them on to the ship. One by one, they were carried into a warm mess room, stripped and then wrapped in thick woollen coats and given hot drinks.

The minesweeper, after setting course for Murmansk, had to make a small detour towards the east during the night. While the survivors of the *Induna* slept, the

Russians came across another boat with survivors; this turned out to be the port lifeboat. There were only nine men remaining in this boat; the two Bofors gunners, five Americans, a fireman and a steward's boy. Shortly after reaching Murmansk, however, on 3 April, one of the Americans and the boy died in hospital.

After some weeks of treatment, six of these were able to walk and were later sent back to England. The remainder, who were kept in hospital at Murmansk, unhappily had such severe frostbite they had to have legs or feet amputated.

From the *Induna*'s total complement of sixty-six only twenty-four survived. For them the tragic history of PQ13 at last came to a close.

CHAPTER SIX

Eastbound Convoy PQ14

With *Trinidad* helpless in dry dock at Rosta, it was of the greatest importance that the steel plates were brought to it in the shortest possible time. On Wednesday 9 April 1942, the next eastward-bound convoy, PQ14, comprising twenty-three merchant ships accompanied by eight anti-submarine trawlers and minesweepers, set sail from Reykjavik in Iceland for Murmansk. Their course lay along the northern coast of Iceland, their intention being to rendezvous with the 10,000-ton cruiser HMS *Edinburgh* (one of two of its type, *Belfast* being the other) and a strong destroyer and corvette escort north-east of the island before proceeding eastward into the Barents Sea.

From the beginning things went wrong. The ice barrier, which at this time of the year would normally have receded to permit an easy passage, was much further south than usual, and on Sunday morning the convoy and its escort found themselves in thick drifting ice. HMS *Edinburgh*, flying the flag of Rear-Admiral Sir Stuart Bonham-Carter, KCB, CB, DSO, and commanded by Captain Hugh Faulkner, later to become Rear-Admiral Faulkner, CB, CBE, DSO, had left Scapa Flow carrying a deck cargo of large steel plates for the damaged *Trinidad*. As she headed for the rendezvous point, she and her escorts ran into thick fog which soon shut down visibility altogether. Only radar kept the vessels from colliding.

The screen showed precisely where each ship was, so that without any alteration in course or speed they were able to proceed on schedule.

But now came disturbing news from the convoy area. Three minesweepers had collided with ice, resulting in torn hulls and leaking compartments; three anti-submarine trawlers reported their asdic-domes severely damaged and unusable; and three others were in such critical condition they were forced to return to Iceland. At the same time the merchant ships themselves had run into the ice field. The great vessels, loaded down to the waterline, were soon colliding with huge tables of ice and in some cases the compacted wall of the ice barrier itself. Hulls buckled, plates were ruptured, stems were crushed and propellers smashed. A poor beginning to a voyage that had so much promise.

When the weather cleared and *Edinburgh* joined the convoy it was discovered that out of the twenty-three merchantmen only eight were present, with their escort of six destroyers, four corvettes, four minesweepers and two trawlers. By Thursday the convoy was just ten miles south of Bear Island, heading east into the Barents Sea and approaching one of the most dangerous areas of the voyage. Any hopes that the convoy might escape detection were shattered when German reconnaissance planes found them, while radar screens and asdics detected concentrations of enemy submarines waiting to the north and south.

Edinburgh could do little to counter that danger or help the destroyers at this point. Her function was to protect the convoy against surface attack from roaming destroyers. It was no place for a large cruiser to be operating, where it would be vulnerable to submarine attack, so, after signalling his decision to the senior officer of the close escorts, Commander Maxwell Richmond, OBE, in the destroyer *Bulldog*, *Edinburgh* positioned herself ten miles astern of the convoy. Assuming full responsibility, Commander Richmond then signalled the commodore of the merchant ships, Captain Edward Rees, DSC, RD, RNR, aboard the vessel *Empire Howard*, to alter course and lead the convoy southwards to avoid the ice field and perhaps an enemy minefield ahead.

The move was executed efficiently, with destroyers and corvettes racing around dropping pattern after pattern of depth charges to keep the enemy's head down and away from the convoy. The convoy was now moving eastward in a formation of four columns of two ships each, with *Empire Howard* in the leading column. At this stage the merchant ships had as close escorts the two anti-submarine trawlers *Northern Wave* and *Lord Middleton* positioned some distance astern, with the destroyer *Beverley* almost a mile ahead, while the remaining destroyers and corvettes formed a protective screen chasing submarine contacts.

However, one U-boat successfully penetrated the screen and, carefully selecting its target, fired three torpedoes. *Empire Howard* was the victim. Unseen, the deadly tin fish plunged into the hull to explode in the boiler room and magazine.

The explosion was enormous, tearing out the centre of the vessel and splitting her in two. The upper decks disappeared and with them the entire cargo of 2000 tons of army trucks which tumbled into the sea in a cacophonous roar which brought the crews of the accompanying ships to the rails to stare in horror and disbelief. With her shattered hull screaming in protest,

Empire Howard began to sink stern first. Within thirty seconds of the explosions the water was up to the bridge. Shouting to the others to leave the ship, the captain, Captain Downie, calmly stepped into the freezing sea wearing a life-jacket. He was barely twenty yards away when the bows of the ship lifted and then slid under. Only sixty seconds had elapsed since the torpedoes struck.

All that could be seen through the drifting black smoke was a great circle of swirling water, bubbling and erupting as air broke through the surface, bringing a mass of flotsam. Then, as the smoke cleared, Captain Downie saw that some of the crew were clinging to bits of wreckage and to three rafts which had floated off as the ship disappeared. In the rolling swell one man swept past him. It was the commodore, Captain Rees, a smile on his lips, calmly trying to smoke a cigar. In the next few seconds a large roller carried him out of sight and he was never seen again. Thus died a brave man, who with rare fortitude faced the inevitable calmly and with dignity.

Such was the freezing temperature of the sea that normally a man in the water would have been dead in a matter of minutes. But by chance the survivors were swimming around in a pool of fuel oil inches thick which had spilled out from the ship's tanks. It was this that kept them alive.

In the meantime the two trawlers astern of the convoy raced towards the stricken vessel, their purpose twofold: to attack the U-boat with depth charges and to rescue survivors. *Northern Wave* was the first to arrive, but its young commanding officer was faced with a harrowing dilemma. At the beginning of his voyage around Iceland the asdic dome under the hull had been so badly damaged by ice floes that he now had no way of confirming if the U-boat was still below and moving around in the middle of the convoy. If he attacked with depth charges it was certain that many of those struggling in the sea in a huge area of black fuel oil and flotsam would be killed from the effects of the terrible concussions. If he did not and the U-boat were to escape there would be another ship sunk, perhaps two or maybe more. Reason argued that the U-boat was still there, since too little time had elapsed for it to escape, but should he turn a blind eye to the submarine in order to save the survivors?

When he was given command of *Northern Wave* his orders had been clear: 'Attack and destroy, the convoy must be saved.' Tortured by the agonizing decision he had to make, the young captain gave the order: 'Fire depth charges.' Set at the exploding depths of 150 feet and 300 feet, ten charges catapulted into the sea. Seconds later, in a series of eruptions which shattered the silence over the water, the charges exploded, bursting into huge fountains of water. Of the men in the sea only those distant from the detonations survived the shock waves. The rest were killed instantly, with broken necks or with horrific internal injuries. As the trawler moved in closer they could be seen bobbing up and down in the swell in a macabre dance of death.

The trawler moved in to begin rescue operations, the engines were stopped and the order given to go full astern; but because of some fault the engines could not be restarted. Already the ship was drifting through an area where some men were still alive and at least six clinging to a raft, and as they neared a line was thrown down. Unfortunately the ship was still moving forward and the raft, still attached, was pulled under the stern and close to the propellors. This brought a new danger, for if the engines should suddenly start and the ship go astern, the blades would cut them to pieces. To avert this the order was given to cast off, and the men on the raft, ignorant of the reason, could only stare in disbelief. As the ship moved further away their relief turned to anger and despair. But soon the second trawler, *Lord Middleton*, arrived and began the work of rescue. It was another fifteen minutes before *Northern Wave* could return and although a boat was launched to try to find more distant survivors no other men were picked up.

Aboard both vessels every effort was made to revive the rescued men. Still conscious, they were in bad condition. Their wet clothes were removed, they were wrapped in blankets, put in the warmest compartments and then given whisky and brandy to restore circulation. Minutes later a message was received from the medical officer of one of the escort destroyers warning that on no account should spirits be given to the survivors. But it was too late, for those who fell asleep would never wake again. The giving of spirits might seem the most natural thing to do, but it can increase hypothermia and lead to heart failure.

Out of *Empire Howard*'s crew of fifty-four only eighteen were rescued, and of these, nine died on board the trawlers. In the hope of finding some evidence of a submarine kill, *Northern Wave* searched the area carefully but found nothing except wreckage and bobbing corpses among the thick oil. With all hope gone of contacting the enemy and the asdic-dome still out of action, the sad and frustrated crew of the trawler set off to rejoin the convoy.

Meanwhile the returning convoy of sixteen ships from Murmansk bound for Iceland, QP10, which left the Kola inlet on 10 April, was heavily attacked on the first three days by U-boats and dive-bombers, resulting in the loss of four empty ships.

To Admiral Bonham-Carter the loss of *Empire Howard* was cause for concern for they were barely halfway through the 2000-mile voyage and entering the danger-ous stretch from Bear Island to the Kola inlet where the Germans would undoubtedly concentrate their forces. His anxiety was justified when a signal was received from intelligence sources in Norway that a force of enemy destroyers had already left Kirkenes in north Norway with the purpose of intercepting the convoy. To counter this threat, *Edinburgh* placed herself ten miles ahead of the convoy and to the south. But the attack failed to materialize, mainly because the German flotilla ran into a force 9 gale with driving snow and were ordered to return to base. A strong force of dive-bombers was now dispatched to attack the convoy, but a heaven-sent blessing arrived in the form of dense fog which hid PQ14 from detection.

On Saturday 19 April, *Edinburgh*, accompanied by the two destroyers *Forester* and *Foresight*, entered the Kola inlet and made its way upstream. At anchor were a number of cargo vessels waiting to join the next convoy westward. For others the stay would be long and arduous. Evidence of enemy action was there for all to see: hulls with gaping holes, crumpled, rusting bridges and distorted girders.

Summing up the overall situation Admiral Bonham-Carter dispatched the following signal to the Admiralty:

Under the present conditions with no hours of darkness, continually under air observation, submarines concentrating in the bottlenecks, torpedo attacks to be expected, our destroyers unable to carry out a proper hunt or search owing to oil situation, serious losses must be expected in every convoy . . . I consider it was due to the fine work of the anti-submarine force that only one ship was lost when several submarines were in the vicinity of the convoy. I wish to bring to the notice of their Lordships the name of the Commanding Officer of *Bulldog*, Commander M. Richmond who was Senior Officer of the close escort. Until enemy aerodromes in north Norway are neutralized I consider convoys to north Russia should be suspended during the months of continuous light unless the very high percentage of losses can be accepted or sufficient air protection can be provided.

That report to the First Sea Lord did not go unheeded. Admiral Pound fully appreciated the perilous conditions under which the convoys had to sail, especially when the continuous daylight allowed the enemy to operate over the whole twenty-four hours. In response to Admiral Sir John Tovey's representations, the Admiralty promised a few more destroyers and corvettes drawn from the Western Approaches Command. But this was simply robbing Peter to pay Paul, since the Atlantic escorts were already far too weak.

The return to Iceland of so many cargo vessels from the luckless PQ14 convoy increased the backlog of supplies waiting to be shipped to north Russia. But it also led the War Cabinet, headed by Winston Churchill as

Minister of Defence, to press for an increase in the size of future convoys. The policy was excellent but its implementation left Sir John Tovey with an almost impossible task. The larger the convoy the greater number of escort ships needed, and these were simply not available. Despite Admiral Tovey's pleas, however, the Admiralty was adamant: future convoys were to be larger, and heavy losses in ships and men was the price that had to be paid.

Immediately following *Edinburgh*'s arrival in the estuary, barges drew alongside to unload the huge steel plates and take them upriver to the stricken *Trinidad*.

During the nine days *Edinburgh* was there a steady stream of badly injured merchant seamen, survivors from bombed or torpedoed ships, was carried aboard the cruiser. These were the worst of many mutilated seamen who miraculously had survived impossible conditions in open boats before reaching land or rescue ships. In many cases legs and arms, deadened by intense frostbite, had turned gangrenous. The one overcrowded hospital in Murmansk had done what it could for them, but amputations had had to be carried out under the most primitive conditions. The Russians could not be blamed. What few medical supplies were available were rapidly exhausted by the increasing demand of their own front line only twenty miles away.

Most of the survivors showed a light of hope in their eyes now that they were shortly bound for home, but in others that light had died. Those with drastic amputations had little will to live knowing that if ever they reached Britain there would be little satisfaction in life, their truncated bodies needing to be tended for the rest of their lives. But all had a story to tell of miraculous survival in impossible Arctic conditions and under fire from every form of destruction the enemy could throw at them.

The stories recounted here were taken from reports given by the survivors and later recorded in official government documents. There was the story related by the captain of a large merchant ship torpedoed near the Great Ice Barrier. He states:

The torpedo struck us on the port side in the engine room. There was a loud explosion as the water was thrown up. I was in the chart room at the time and rushed on to the bridge. Looking aft I saw that the port motor boat was hanging in two pieces from the davits and I noticed a large number of men on the after boat deck, including gunners, firemen and sailors. They were endeavouring to lower the only remaining lifeboat and had just succeeded in bringing the boat to the water line with a number of men in it when a second torpedo struck the ship on the starboard side. The men in the lifeboat and those on the boat deck were all killed instantly by flying debris. After giving the order to abandon ship the officers lowered my small dinghy and I collected my brief case and made my way to it. I found several of the officers already in the dinghy along with some of the crew and discovered there were thirteen in her. Unfortunately the boat then fouled the wreckage of the motor boat, which upset the dinghy, throwing us all in the water. The Second and Third Officers managed to grab the lifelines hanging from the deck and regain the ship. The Chief Officer who had his duffel coat on was floating but unable to swim owing to water collecting in the sleeves and hood of his coat. I heard him shouting for help but owing to the weight of the case on my back and the freezing water it was all I could do to keep myself afloat and struggle to the upturned boat.

Several members of the crew had got away on four rafts and some clinging to the dinghy managed to swim to one of these rafts. A few minutes later, a third torpedo struck the ship penetrating the hold where the explosives were stored. There was an enormous explosion amidships and when the smoke and debris had cleared, I saw that the ship had broken in two and in a second or two she disappeared. One of the Transport Officers swam over to the upturned dinghy and together we climbed on to the keel and tried to right it.

We managed to roll the boat over but she came too far and capsized again. We tried a second time and this time managed to right the boat which was by now about one foot under water. We stood on the forward end, and a few feet of the after end lifted out of the water. I emptied my brief case and used it as a bailer and after a struggle managed to reduce the water level in the boat and we climbed in. We rowed amongst the wreckage and picked up one of the signalmen. A few minutes later a submarine broke surface while the periscope of another sub was sighted at some distance. The submarine came alongside one of the rafts and a seaman was taken aboard and asked the ship's name. Having given the information he was handed a bottle of water and some bread and after taking a photograph of the survivors on the raft, the submarine captain told them the course and the distance to north Russia.

It was very cold in the boat as the water was at freezing point and all the survivors were wet through. Whilst rowing around I came across the upturned lifeboat but decided it was impossible to right it without assistance from the men on the rafts. I told all the rafts to paddle over towards the lifeboat but when they arrived they were too cold and numb to do anything about it. One man with his brains knocked out died on the raft so I buried him. The Second Engineer also died from injuries received on board and he was also buried. Some time later a ship was sighted on the horizon. We burnt flares to attract attention and at midnight HMS Lotus came over and picked us up and two days later we arrived in north Russia, most of us suffering from intense frostbite in the feet and legs.

There were several members of my crew who played an heroic part in this tragedy. The Chief Steward remained behind after the ship was abandoned although he heard the order, attending to the injured. He further assisted in rescuing the Second Engineer from the engine room and having put him on a stretcher carried him on to the raft. Whilst doing this the third torpedo struck and the Chief Steward went down with the ship but managed to swim to the raft. The Second Cook also stayed behind and assisted in the rescue of the Second Engineer. After completing this rescue he went round the ship distributing lifejackets to other members of the crew who had lost theirs but when the third torpedo struck he was killed by falling debris and went down with the ship. My Chief Engineer also behaved magnificently, firstly in leading the rescue party to the Second Engineer who was trapped in the engine room in spite of knowing that the order had been given to abandon ship. Although badly injured in the leg he carried on with the rescue work showing great bravery and finally just managed to get away from the ship in time. The rescued Second Engineer had already been on three trips to Russia with me and volunteered for this fourth trip. This time he was not so fortunate and was trapped in the engine room as the two torpedoes struck, one from either side. Although badly injured in the legs and spine, with the aid of the rescuers he was hauled up and put on to one of the rafts but as the third torpedo struck he was blown into the sea. He managed to cling to some wreckage and was eventually pulled back on to the raft where he died from his injuries and exposure. Outstanding courage was shown by the Senior Wireless Operator also, who despite the order to abandon ship succeeded in getting his messages away and remained at his station until satisfied that the messages had got through. I'm glad to say he managed to escape on one of the rafts.

Then there was the story of another captain who survived the torpedoing of his ship when thirty-nine of his crew of fifty-nine lost their lives:

We had been repeatedly attacked by enemy aircraft and I made a course for the north-east which brought us up against the ice barrier and by taking cover in the fog banks managed to avoid being spotted by other aircraft searching for us. Later the weather cleared. The sea was fairly rough and at about 4 p.m. that day, we were hit by a torpedo on the port side under the bridge. As I rushed out on to the bridge I was struck by falling debris and was unconscious for a few minutes. Just as I came round I heard another explosion as a second torpedo plunged into the engine room. The port boat which was in the process of being lowered was blown away. About one minute later there was a third explosion in the after end of the vessel. I think the ammunition store in the after hold must have exploded as I saw a great column of smoke rising and could smell cordite. The ship immediately broke into three pieces; the main mast crashed down and one man who was lowering the forward fall of the lifeboat was blown away and the boat left hanging by the after fall. The explosion also destroyed the starboard lifeboat. Three rafts were managed to be released from the ship and I threw a knife to one of the crew and told him to cut the after fall of the hanging lifeboat. This boat then crashed into the sea and immediately became waterlogged. There was only one man left on board with me and we both jumped into the sea. The bridge was then about 5 feet above water and one minute later the vessel disappeared. I swam with this sailor to the water-logged boat where there was already one man and having climbed in we found that the water was up above our waists. We picked up several other members of the crew and finally there were 17 of us in the boat. Before the fog shut down visibility altogether I saw 7 men on one raft and 14 on another. We did everything possible to get the boat cleared of water which at the time was 0 degrees centigrade but the crew became extremely cold and numb.

Four men died during the first five hours and we were unable to do anything for them. I took the lifejackets off their bodies and buried them. Some time later the weather moderated and the fog lifted. We found a bucket, and with this and the pump, we managed to get the water down to the level of the buoyancy tanks. One by one the men died from exposure and shock until there were only four of us left alive. About this time a large submarine surfaced with U13 painted in black on the side of the conning tower and round this number was painted a black horseshoe. The U-boat closed into my boat and its commander asked me if the ship's captain was a survivor and I told him 'No', as there was the distinct possibility they would take me prisoner. The submarine then went over to the raft and the men on it were asked the same question to which they replied that they thought the ship's captain had gone down with the vessel. The U-boat commander then spoke to my Chief Officer and was asked if he was a Bolshevik and on learning that he was not, said, 'Then what the hell are you going to Russia for?' The Chief Officer was then given the course and distance to Novaya Zemlya, also a bottle of wine, another of gin and five loaves of black bread. The sub had a machine gun trained on us during the conversation and was taking cine-photographs of the men on the rafts as they were receiving the food etc.

The commander who was about 6 ft tall and with

a red beard, spoke English fluently. After about five minutes the submarine submerged and moved off. We rigged the sail and steered a course to the southeast and towards the land which I estimated about 20 miles distant. Later we picked up 9 men from one of the rafts and about 10 o'clock that night with 13 men in the boat we landed on a small island off the coast of Novaya Zemlya. We found the island uninhabited so on landing we rigged our sail as a tent, lit a fire and made some pemmican soup to warm us. We found a number of birds' eggs which we put into the soup and despite the eggs containing young birds it tasted good.

We rested for two days and then climbing some high ground we sighted a vessel which appeared to be stopped. We launched our boat and sailed towards this ship which proved to be American and was aground. Having boarded her we found 7 men from one of the rafts already aboard thus making a total of 20 survivors out of our crew of 68. We remained on board and a week later a Russian survey ship arrived which brought us back to north Russia.

And there were stories like that of the bosun of the *Empire Ranger* and the cabin boy. After being dive-bombed, the ship sank quickly and only one lifeboat managed to get away. Thirty-eight survivors were packed into this boat. For six days they were carried along by wind and tide, in snowstorms, gales and the freezing wind. Each day took its toll. By the sixth day the boat was full of frozen corpses, and in the bows sat an elderly seaman, his beard white with snow and frost, looking out across the tumbling sea, frozen solid and quite dead. Only two of the original thirty-eight were found to be still alive. One was the cabin boy, David, a Scot from Edinburgh. Stretched across him, providing warmth and protecting him from the snow and wind, lay the bosun, more dead than alive. Although the boy's feet were in a dreadful state from frostbite through long immersion in ice-cold water in the boat, he eventually recovered. But the bosun's bid to save the boy's life extracted a terrible penalty. The Russian hospital into which he was later admitted found that to save his life it was necessary to amputate both arms and legs.

The bosun revealed later that on the fifth day of their ill-fated voyage, when only four men remained alive, nature had played an almost unbelievable and cruel trick. Swirling mist had descended, fanned by a bitter wind. As the fog thickened it blanketed visibility altogether, shutting out all sound. Only the ceaseless lapping of water against the boat could be heard. Then suddenly they heard a whistle. The sound faded then rose again, louder and more constant. Their hearts raced with excitement. Surely it was someone from a rescue boat trying to locate them. With what little strength was left they tried to shout, but there was no answer. Still the whistle persisted. First it seemed to be ahead and then astern. The sound was eerie, almost supernatural. In their low state of mind the mystery, deepening every minute, became almost frightening. Minutes later their hopes were dashed as the riddle was solved. On the thwart, gently rolling with the movement of the sea, lay an empty bottle. When the wind swept through the boat it played on the open end of the bottle, trilling the whistling sound. As the bosun said later, it was a moment when hope turned to despair, optimism to despondency, the worst moment of their ordeal.

CHAPTER SEVEN

The Cargo of Gold Bullion

The time was now nearing for *Edinburgh*'s departure, and two days before she left the safety of the Kola inlet she took aboard a cargo which forty years later was to attract worldwide interest. Supply Petty Officer Arthur Start in an interview described exactly what happened:

I had been asleep for about an hour when I was awakened by the bugler sounding off, 'Both watches of the duty hands fall in, in the starboard waist'. My messmate sat up with a start, looked at his watch and said – 'What the 'ell's goin' on – it's quarter to bloody midnight'. When we arrived on deck we could hardly believe our eyes. The scene was like something from a film. Secured along the starboard side were two barges and at vantage points aboard were about a score of Russian soldiers armed with 'Tommy' guns held at the ready. On our own ship, stationed at regular intervals from the deck and up the ladders to the flight deck were also our own Royal Marines keeping guard. As we watched, a tarpaulin covering the barge's cargo was drawn back to reveal scores of ammunition boxes. The natural assumption at first was that these contained small arms ammunition – but why should there be such security for a routine job? Then in a matter of minutes the truth was out. The boxes contained not ammunition but gold – gold bullion. Over five tons of it to be stored in the cruiser and shipped to the United Kingdom. The boxes, rope handled, were extremely heavy, each needing two men to lift them. In the dull grey daylight of the Arctic midnight we carried those boxes all the way up to the flight deck and there lowered them by ropes through a shaft trunking to the bomb room three decks below.

All the time we were unloading the gold there seemed to be an aura of evil present. An uncomfortable feeling of impending disaster. We all felt it – most expressed it. Superstition is a strong characteristic with sailors throughout the world. The ominous feeling persisted and when part way through the operation sleet started falling and the heavy red stencilling on the boxes ran freely to drip a trail of scarlet along the snow-covered decks, apprehension redoubled. One seaman expressed the thoughts of all of us when passing an officer he said – 'It's going to be a bad trip, sir, this is Russian gold dripping with blood'. They were prophetic words indeed.

The value of the bullion was in the region of £5 million; forty years later its value would be £45 million. The gold was a down payment from the Russians to the United States Treasury for the thousands of tons of war material delivered at Murmansk and Archangel to equip the Red Army. Had *Edinburgh*'s crew known the gold's history of blood and death they would have been even more apprehensive. Each bar, stamped with the old czar's double headed eagle, had been accumulated by him in the days before the Russian Revolution.

The gold bullion had been transported from Moscow to the port of Murmansk via a 1000-mile-long single-line rail track, a perilous and dangerous route in some places passing within fifty miles of the front line where the Russians were trying to hold back the combined weight of the German and Finnish armies. It was the lifeline of their supplies to and from the north and a constant target. Formerly an insignificant local line, the single track had now assumed the utmost importance in the defence of the 2000-mile-long battle front from Murmansk to Leningrad and southwards to Rostov by the Black Sea. The railway snakes across the Kola Peninsula for 150 miles, skirting the multitude of lakes which dominate the landscape there. This brings it to the port of Kandalaksha at the western extremity of the White Sea. This was the most vulnerable stretch of the line, running as it does between the natural boundary of the sea and the Finnish frontier only fifty miles to the west. From there the line continues for a further 250 miles, running south-east along the southern coast of the White Sea to the town of Belomorsk. There it turns south for 500 miles, holding a course parallel to the Finnish border at a distance of 150 miles. The much-threatened stretch that ran between the great lakes of Onega and Ladoga was known as the Karelian front. The line then ended at rail junctions in the vicinity of Leningrad, from where the trains could be re-routed to their final destinations.

The Finns had succeeded in cutting the railway in the vicinity of Lake Onega in August 1941. The Russians had then to construct a loop running east from Belomorsk to join up with the line between Archangel and Moscow. Superhuman effort on the part of the engineering and

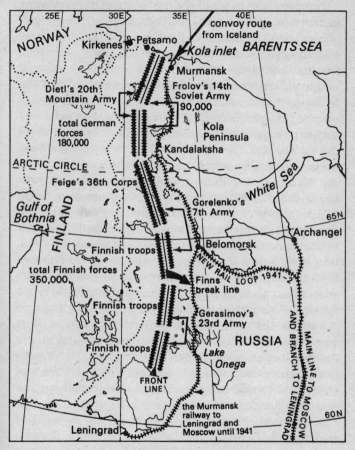

The Battle for the Murmansk Railway

rail construction gangs in the face of appalling conditions experienced on the southern coast of the White Sea in winter enabled the new line to open in a very short time and supply trains once more to get south with their invaluable freights.

One of the most important sources of raw material for Germany was the rich nickel ore mining area of Petsamo on the Barents Sea coast of northern Finland. Ore-carrying ships operated a shuttle service around North Cape, then south down the Norwegian coast to German ports. This traffic was harassed by British submarines. The nickel ore, together with Swedish iron ore, was vital to the German war effort, and supplies had to be maintained whatever the cost. The German occupation of Denmark and Norway secured both the Baltic and their northern flank and thereby greatly improved the safety of the ore traffic. However, the Führer was still obsessed with the threat of an Allied invasion of Norway, which would provide them with a land route to Russia. If this happened, Germany would inevitably lose the Petsamo mines. He therefore formed the Army of Lapland, later to be known as the German 20th Mountain Army. These 180,000 troops were under the command of General Dietl, whose task was to hold the Petsamo area and operate alongside his ally, Finland, which had been at war with Russia since 1939.

The introduction of convoys to north Russia had stiffened the Russian resistance, so that the German advances on the Eastern Front had slowed down. While Hitler was doing everything possible to stop the convoys, he also had to cut the rail link, and the stretch in the Kandalaksha area was the place to do it. As early as December 1940 operational plans for the strike had been drawn up. Once again, Hitler over-ruled his general staff and odered Dietl to take Murmansk, secure the whole Kola Peninsula and cut the line as well. If successful this operation, known as 'Silver Fox', would not only terminate the flow of Allied aid but could be the start of an outflanking movement round the Russian armies further south.

On paper it looked a straightforward task, as the German and Finnish forces together totalled over half a million men, outnumbering the Russians by two to one. But wars are not fought on paper; the three widely separated German thrusts eastward were a failure. The Russian army units, though outnumbered, had the advantages of strong artillery, short lines of communication and well-prepared positions. The weakness of the whole German strategy in Finland lay in poor communications and supply; there were very few roads and only one single-track railway serving the central area. Elsewhere pack mules supplied the troops. The direct sea route to Finland through the Baltic was unusable in winter when the Gulf of Bothnia froze up, while at all times there was a lack of German merchant ships.

In the spring of 1942, the 14th Soviet Army under the command of Lieutenant-General Frolov held the northern sector that included the approaches to Murmansk and the Kola Peninsula. In June the previous year, Frolov had had only two rifle divisions and a hastily formed third, made up of conscripted civilians and sailors. These were thrown into the defence of the port and, though inexperienced, were enough to stop the Germans a few miles from the town. By the following April he was strong enough to attack Petsamo with the Russian navy supporting him. However, he was repulsed, and from then on the front remained static, apart from a number of localized actions by the Luftwaffe which destroyed locomotives, derailed trains and smashed up the line. However, Russian repair gangs, working round the clock, made good the damage as soon as it was inflicted and kept supplies rolling south.

Had the Germans succeeded in cutting the railway line at Kandalaksha and infiltrating the Kola Peninsula, the convoys would have had to be diverted to Archangel. This would probably have put an end to them, as it would have added a further 300 miles to the voyage and restricted the convoys to summer passages only.

But to return to *Edinburgh*. On the morning of 28 April, with the gold safely stacked deep in the bowels of the ship, the cruiser left the Kola inlet to escort convoy QP11, made up of thirteen merchant ships, to Iceland. Seven of these were British: *Briarwood*, *Dan-y-Bryn*, *Trehatta*, *Atheltemplar*, *Gallant Fox*, *Ballot* and *Dunboyne*. Five were American: *West Cheswald*, *Stone Street*, *El Dina*, *El Estra* and the *Moonmadmer*. And one was Russian: *Ciolkovsky*. Apart from *Edinburgh*, the escort was made up of six destroyers, *Bulldog* (Commander Maxwell Richmond, DSO, MBE, RN), *Beagle* (Commander Ralph Medley, RN), *Foresight* (Commander Jocelyn Stuart Salter, RN), *Forester* (Lieutenant-Commander George Huddart, RN), *Amazon* (Lieutenant-Commander Nigel Roper, RN), and *Beverley* (Commander John Grant, RN); four corvettes, *Oxlip* (Lieutenant-Commander Alfred Collinson, RN), *Saxifrage* (Lieutenant-Commander E. Chapman, RN), *Campanula* (Lieutenant-Commander Alfred Hine, RN) and *Snowflake* (Lieutenant-Commander Sidney Cuthbertson, RN); and two Russian destroyers.

The destroyer and corvette force commanded by Commander Richmond was equal to combating U-boat attacks but none was capable of dealing with the larger and much more heavily armed Narvik class destroyers which might be expected to engage them from bases in Norway. That would be *Edinburgh*'s function. She had four triple turrets of 6-inch guns, twelve 4-inch and twenty smaller guns. The armed cruiser steamed patiently along behind the 6-knot convoy, its crew keenly aware not only of their responsibility to protect the merchant ships but of the importance of safely delivering the vast fortune of shining gold they carried. Deep in the bowels of the ship the asdic machine pinged the depths, searching for the approach of submarines.

On the morning of Wednesday 29 April a German reconnaissance plane found them and reported back to Norway. At such an early stage of their homeward-bound voyage, detection could well be a portent of heavy attacks. It brought a measure of anxiety to Admiral Bonham-Carter. At the German headquarters at Kirkenes the incoming reports were received with satisfaction by the 'Admiral Arctic', Admiral Hubert Schmundt, who was given permission by German Navy Group North to dispatch three heavily armed Narvik class destroyers to intercept QP11. At the same time signals were dispatched to seven of his U-boats to close in on the convoy. He had two objectives: to attack and destroy the merchant vessels and their escorts, and to overwhelm and sink the glittering prize, HMS *Edinburgh*.

The intelligence report stated that the convoy was proceeding steadily north. That was no problem; Schmundt was prepared to wait, knowing that in a few hours the British convoy's course would have to be altered. When the convoy reached the ice barrier it would have to turn westward. The only problem for German Naval Command was that its forays into the Arctic Ocean to attack convoys were limited by reason of decreasing supplies of oil fuel. One of Hitler's reasons for attacking Russia was to acquire the Caucasian oilfields to sustain his vast war machine. When the winter battle before Moscow reduced these hopes, the Romanian oilfields were his only source of supply, and they were not sufficient to sustain the Russian campaign. He had hoped that by the winter of 1941–2 he would have acquired control of the Caucasian oilfields, but the rugged resistance of the Russian armies prevented him from achieving this objective and his planned campaign had to be limited.

The rationing of oil fuel fell most heavily on the navy, as priority had to be given to tanks and planes. In the spring of 1942 supplies had been reduced from 46,000 tons to 8000 tons and as a result German Navy Group issued the following order:

> All operations to be discontinued including those by light forces. The sole exceptions are operations made necessary by enemy action.

From this time on, any naval engagement was influenced purely by the importance of the operation, where the possibility of success justified the cost in fuel. In the light of this order Schmundt was not prepared to send his ships chasing all over the Barents Sea after the British convoy. Instead he would let them come to him. After ordering his U-boats to take up positions across the convoy route and three of his destroyer group to be made ready to put to sea, he waited. The three were the

Hermann Schoemann, under Lieutenant-Commander Heinrich Wittig, Z24, under Lieutenant-Commander Martin Salzwedel, and Z25, under Lieutenant-Commander Heinz Peters, all under the direct command of Captain Schulze-Hinrichs.

The convoy's course northwards was constantly interrupted by drifting ice fields and frequent sightings of German submarines which kept the destroyer escorts constantly on the alert, constantly on the move dropping depth charges. As sightings and contacts increased it was realized that this was no place for a cruiser to be ambling along at the 6-knot speed of the convoy, and the admiral gave the order to Captain Faulkner to take *Edinburgh* some twenty miles to the north-west in a stand-off position and to zigzag her course to avoid U-boat attacks.

After signalling *Bulldog* of the decision, *Edinburgh* made off until she was beyond sight over the horizon. Although undoubtedly an astute move, witnesses in the cruiser and in some of the destroyers were mystified because she had not ordered one of the destroyers to accompany her to act as a screen against possible submarine attacks. As Captain Richmond watched the cruiser disappear he must have been keenly aware of the heavy responsibility now placed upon him. His group of escorts would be no match for the big German destroyers if they found him. Although there was some comfort in knowing that *Edinburgh* was somewhere ahead, there could be no certainty from which direction the enemy might approach.

It was just at the end of her twenty-mile patrol amid frequent snow flurries, at 4.00 p.m., that disaster overtook the cruiser. Waiting submerged across *Edinburgh*'s path lay U-boat 456 commanded by Lieutenant Max

Teichert. As Teichert watched through the periscope he saw that the cruiser was, incredibly, unaccompanied. Hardly daring to trust his eyes, he searched the horizon in every direction, but there was definitely no escort in sight. Such opportunities were rare and not to be missed. As the cruiser neared he took careful calculations, knowing he had only two torpedoes left. After a final check he gave the order, and the torpedoes sped on their way towards the unsuspecting *Edinburgh*.

Aboard the cruiser the ship's company carried on with their duties, blissfully unaware of the catastrophe that was about to overtake them. In fact, part of the ship's company had just obeyed the pipe 'Non-duty hands to tea'. Out of the whole complement of over 700, including the admiral, captain, officers and men, only one man anticipated the disaster. This was the asdic operator, who clearly saw on his screen a blip which he identified as a U-boat. In a voice tense with excitement he instantly reported to the bridge, but the admiral considered the echo must be a mistake. The operator insisted, reporting that this echo was firm and strong and must be a submerged submarine. Still not believing the report, the young man was brusquely ordered to 'disregard'.

But the operator had made no mistake, the echo was indeed a submarine. As the torpedoes homed in on their target, *Edinburgh* sailed on, oblivious of the silver wakes of the steel fish flashing through the black waters. Both torpedoes were on target. The first hit the cruiser amidships, ploughing into the forward boiler room, destroying many compartments, killing everybody in the explosion area and flooding mess decks in a cascade of oil and water. The second smashed into the stern blowing the reinforced steel quarter-deck upwards like a sheet of cardboard to fold itself around the barrels of the three 6-inch guns of Y turret. At the same time the rudder and two of the four great propellors were smashed away. Such was the enormity of the blast it blew the bottom plates of the ship down to create a sort of twisted fin or rudder.

Amid the dreadful thunder of tons of sea water cascading into the ship and the scream of rending metal, the cruiser slowed to a stop, listing to starboard. In a matter of seconds this proud warship, which had once been the grudging admiration of cruiser squadrons, had become a mangled sarcophagus of steel, a tomb of smashed bodies with two huge gaping wounds through which poured the icy waters of the Barents Sea. Below decks, in the ensuing darkness, men stumbled and tripped, colliding with one another in a bid to find some way out. In the submerged submarine, Teichert viewed the devastation with satisfaction. If he had had only one more torpedo he could have applied the final death blow, but as it was he could only watch and report the result of his attack back to Norway.

Just two examples of the chaos that existed below decks where the torpedoes exploded will suffice to convey what a living nightmare it was. Leading Stoker Bradley later recalled:

> Just before the torpedo struck I happened to go into the stoker's messdeck which was fairly crowded at the time and was talking to a friend of mine, a young amateur boxer called Harrington. As we chatted, the torpedo exploded in the oil tank below us. The whole messdeck split in two and as the lights went out, Harrington and I and at least another 50

men fell straight through into the storage tank which was partially filled. The emergency light failed to come on and we were down there in complete darkness, floundering around in oil and water. In the blackness with men around screaming and shouting, I managed at last to get a footing and started to make my way towards where I thought the hatch might be. As I moved, I heard Taff Harrington near me. I called out 'Taff' and he grabbed me. The oil was now pouring in fast from burst pipes in adjoining tanks and rising to our shoulders.

Harrington tried to hold my hand but it slipped and he died in the oil. There was another boy called Harrison clinging to a stanchion. I tried to lift him above the level of the oil but he screamed blue murder for he had broken both collar bones and an ankle. All this time I was swallowing oil. Gradually the oil found its level and stopped rising. Everything went very quiet. The hatch above us was sealed and we had no idea if the ship was afloat, partly submerged or at the bottom of the ocean. We must have been there nearly an hour when the miracle happened. The hatch was prized open and three stokers came down with torches and ropes and pulled us to safety. Above, on the fo'c'sle deck outside the galley, Engine Room Artificer Robert Sherriff was standing talking to the Chief Cook, 'Dolly' Gray. The explosion split the deck open where they were standing and both fell through. Sherriff managed to cling to a projecting ledge and regain the deck but the Chief Cook was propelled on downward and was never seen again.

In another compartment several trapped men were saved through the efforts of Supply Petty Officer Arthur Start and his mate Petty Officer Bob Walkey. Start recalled:

> I was in the PO's mess at the time the first torpedo hit. All the lights went out but fortunately I happened to have a torch in my pocket. Chief Petty Officers and Petty Officers came running from everywhere and as I had the only torch, I led them up to the flight deck where in such an event we had been told to muster. Realizing that the messdecks below might still contain trapped men, we lifted back the hatch cover of the vertical shaft down through which the gold had been lowered. Sure enough, within the compartment we could see men swimming around in the oil and water. My mate ran to fetch ropes and ladders but while he was away, several of the men below managed to get into the shaft which was only two feet square. Within the trunking there were no ridges or ledges to provide a hold but in desperation those men managed to come up through by working their knees and backs against the sides. Eventually the hatch was sealed. There were several men down there but they were dead anyway.

From the bridge parapet the admiral, captain and officers gazed down at the starboard side almost in disbelief. A cloud of fire and black smoke erupted from an area along the waterline flowing aft across the decks. *Edinburgh* had been ripped open as if with a giant can opener and the scene aft represented nothing less than a scrapyard. Although Y turret was still there it was entombed in a massive obscene sculpture, silhouetted tall and stark against the cold Arctic light. Sixty-three feet of the stern was nothing but a tangled mass of wreckage. Below, tragedy and heroism walked hand in hand as men trapped in sealed compartments were hauled to safety in the nick of time when bulkheads split open and tons of oil poured in to engulf them, while stokers caught in the blast of ruptured steam pipes had their flesh peeled from their bones and others were trapped alive in unreachable compartments.

As Captain Faulkner climbed quickly down the bridge ladder to reach the flight deck he was met by several hundred of the ship's crew awaiting orders. Many, oil-drenched, had obviously barely escaped the holocaust below. They stood dazed, silent. It was no time for speeches. He paused to tell them that if all went well he had every hope of getting them back to Murmansk. But as his gaze wandered aft at the twisted remains of his once proud ship, his features, normally cheerful, were grim and stern. Then, almost abruptly, he said: 'The Admiral has accepted full responsibility.' With that and a brief salute he hurried aft. Captain Faulkner's only concern was the safety of the ship and of his men. If all watertight doors and hatches were securely locked and the one remaining engine room could be made to function then the chances of returning to the Kola inlet were good.

Meanwhile the convoy, many miles to the north and steadily moving westward, was beset with its own problems. German submarines had been sighted astern and ahead, and Commander Richmond in *Bulldog* was scurrying around with the other escorts depth-charging in a frantic effort to repel attack. It was during all this activity that he received a signal from *Edinburgh* reporting she had been torpedoed. Although reluctant to spare any of his escort ships at this time, he ordered Commander Salter of *Foresight* to take *Forester* and the two Russian destroyers to assist the stricken cruiser. It was 17.30 before they sighted *Edinburgh*, to find with some relief that its one working propellor was enabling some forward movement to be achieved. As they closed they could see that the ship was indeed in a sorry state. The great hole in her side revealed twisted and ruptured compartments almost through to the other side, while damage to what was left of the stern was equally hideous. The smashed propeller shafts hung low in the water, making the ship unmanageable.

The arduous task of towing *Edinburgh* back to Murmansk 250 miles away now began. With the possibility of further U-boat attacks always there, *Foresight* and the two Russian destroyers screened the cruiser while *Forester* passed a towline to the fo'c'sle: It proved a most difficult exercise. The decks were a sheet of ice making it almost impossible to stand. But at last it was accomplished and *Forester* began to tow. The cruiser had become a dead weight, however, and the wire, unable to meet the strain, snapped like a sprung coil, whipping back to wrap itself around rails and bollards. After another four unsuccessful attempts the struggle to tow from the fo'c'sle was abandoned.

Part of the difficulty was that the wreckage aft, hanging down in the water, acted as a rudder and made the cruiser yaw away, so another idea was tried. *Foresight* succeeded in passing a wire from her own fo'c'sle into *Edinburgh*'s stern, allowing the destroyer to operate as a rudder and keep her on course. At the same time, the cruiser added whatever forward movement she could under her own steam. The plan proved reasonably successful, and through that night and the early hours of 1 May movement was made towards the Kola inlet at 3 knots, a slow walking pace. However, at 06.00 the two Russian destroyers signalled that they were short of fuel and would have to return to Murmansk. It was indeed a setback, and the admiral decided that with only the two destroyers to support him both would have to be employed to act as a screen against further U-boat attacks. He was right to be worried, for Teichert in the submerged U456 was following from a safe distance, reporting on the efforts being made to save the cruiser to German Naval Headquarters.

As the two Russian destroyers disappeared in a sweeping snowstorm, the tow was cast off and *Foresight* and *Forester* began a screening operation around the cruiser. *Edinburgh*, however, was almost uncontrollable, and again started yawing, sometimes going round in circles. Only the skilled seamanship of Captain Faulkner enabled these deviations to be checked and some sort of forward motion sustained. Another worry developed when it was seen that the cruiser was leaving in her wake a broad band of oil which would reveal her course to the enemy. An attack was the last thing *Edinburgh* needed at this time. Moreover, a signal from the Senior British Naval Officer at Murmansk reported that enemy submarines had taken up positions across the path to the Kola inlet, and there was another signal, from *Bulldog*, to the effect that Admiralty intelligence had reported that enemy destroyers had left Kirkenes to intercept the convoy or *Edinburgh* or perhaps both. These utterly pessimistic reports were partly offset by another signal from SBNO, Murmansk, that a Russian tug and the

British minesweepers *Harrier, Niger, Hussar* and *Gossamer* were on their way to help them. While this was some consolation, it was clear that their single 4-inch guns would be of little use against the powerful modern 6-inch guns of the Narvik class destroyers, and even the two British destroyers would be outgunned if the enemy should come upon them.

Aboard the cruiser the crew were kept constantly at action stations. For those men in exposed conditions it was sheer hell, with temperatures at 10° below zero. The freezing wind from the polar ice cap numbed their muscles and their senses. Cooked hot meals were out of the question, the only food available being sandwiches and ship's cocoa. From the bridge parapet the admiral and the captain, muffled and hooded, looked out across the cold grey sea with troubled eyes. Could they save this wounded ship, its crew and the vast fortune of gold? With another 200 miles to go, at a speed now reduced to 2 knots, it would take another four days and nights before they reached the shelter of land.

As though *Edinburgh* had not enough troubles, she received a further signal from London that the pocket battleship *Admiral Scheer* had sailed from Trondheim for the Arctic. This vessel was a sister ship of the notorious *Graf Spee* which, after a running battle with British cruisers in 1939, had been scuttled and sunk at Montevideo. *Scheer* was a formidable battleship, with six 11-inch guns, eight 6-inch, and six 4-inch. *Edinburgh*, with most of her guns out of action, would be a sitting target.

CHAPTER EIGHT

The Defence of QP11

At German Naval Headquarters in Norway Admiral Schmundt was highly satisfied with the course of events. Without any damage to his own forces, the powerful British cruiser *Edinburgh* had been erased as a fighting force, and without it the convoy 200 miles to the north-west was virtually defenceless against the powerful German destroyer flotilla. The wheel of fortune had swung his way and presented him with a prize beyond his dreams.

In theory his plan of attack was simple enough. The heavy Narvik class destroyers with their superior arma-ment would liquidate the weak British escorts then, taking their time, would sink the merchant ships. They could then return across the Barents Sea to intercept the crippled cruiser and destroy her.

Very early on the morning of 1 May the German destroyers set a course northwards towards the convoy. Teichert, reporting from U456, had indicated that *Edin-burgh* could be attacked and destroyed at any time for she was barely moving, whereas the westward-bound convoy might soon be outside the limit of operations.

Nine hours later, at 13.30, the German destroyers came upon the convoy and prepared to attack. Mean-while *Bulldog* had received the signal from the Admiralty that the enemy might be heading north to attack QP11, and Commander Richmond had closed the escorts around the merchant ships in a protective screen. During this manoeuvre masses of drifting ice were seen across their path, extending fifteen miles southward. He had little choice but to order the convoy to swing south-west, but at the same time he mobilized the merchant ships in among the ice floes to protect the starboard flank and minimize the number of directions from which the German ships might attack.

At 13.45 the enemy began shelling the convoy. Immediately signalling *Edinburgh* that the enemy were attacking, *Bulldog* raced at full speed across the front of the convoy, signalling *Amazon*, *Beverley* and *Beagle* to join her. In a defensive move the four British destroyers led by Richmond blazed away at the enemy with their 4.7-inch guns. In theory the British ships should have been annihilated, but despite their advantage the Germans kept turning away or doubling back. Each time this happened the British ships turned also, always keeping themselves between the convoy and the enemy.

Suddenly *Amazon* was hit by a salvo that enveloped her in a sheet of flame and smoke, but still maintaining her line she raced on at top speed. Her commanding officer Lieutenant Roper, wounded from the explosions, gazed down from the bridge to see that the forward gun had been torn out of its mounting with its crew lying dead or wounded on the deck. Aft, two other guns had been smashed with their crews killed and the steering positions made useless. The ship was now out of control, careering along at 30 knots, while the other British destroyers doubled back on the previous course in line with the enemy. By a supreme effort to control her steering, *Amazon* was able to join the others at the rear

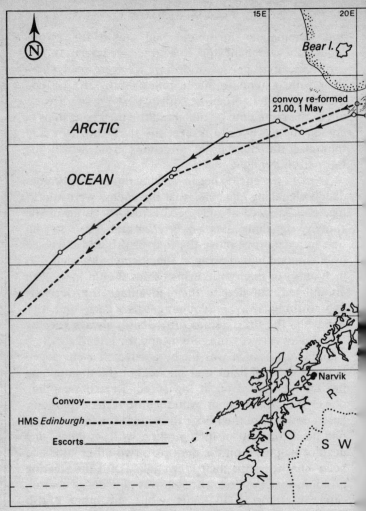

Convoy QP11 to Iceland, 28 April to 2 May 1942

Bulldog and escorts
fight off attack
by *Schoemann*, Z24 and Z25

several U-boat
sightings

torpedo bombers
attack

Edinburgh torpedoed by
U456. 16.13, 30 April.
Attempts return to Murmansk

74 N

barrier

ice floes

05.40, 1 May

German destroyers head SE
to intercept *Edinburgh*

73 N

altered course,
20.30, 29 April

72 N

German destroyers

BARENTS SEA

North Cape

Edinburgh sunk 05.50,
2 May, 71.51N, 35.10E

first ice

71 N

Banak

reconnaisance
aircraft

Tromso

Kirkenes

70 N

Petsamo

22.05, 28 April

Kola inlet

Murmansk

69 N

FINLAND   R U S S I A

EN

ARCTIC CIRCLE

25E   30E   35E

of the column, making it appear to the German ships that she was still a formidable fighting unit. At last, unable to penetrate the protective screen, they turned away.

An hour later the German ships reappeared. *Bulldog* promptly turned and headed directly for them at full speed, with clouds of spray pluming over the fo'c'sle deck. The sight of this intrepid little ship speeding in on them with all guns blazing must have been quite intimidating, for after firing a few torpedoes they turned and made off. This lion-hearted attack by *Bulldog* was not unlike Sir Richard Grenville's in 1591, when he charged his little flagship *Revenge* into the Spanish galleons.

Meanwhile, however, torpedoes fired by the enemy, now at the end of their course, were surfacing and running in among the ice floes towards the merchant ships. One ploughed into the Russian freighter *Ciolkovsky*, and in minutes her bows settled, her stern rose high and she disappeared. At 15.30 the enemy returned, striking from the east. Again the British destroyers rushed into the attack, with *Bulldog* receiving the full weight of the German's armament yet miraculously escaping a direct hit. Frustrated in this further attempt the enemy once more turned away. Again and again that afternoon, six times in all, they returned to the attack, but on each occasion were beaten off by the determined resistance of the little British ships led by Richmond.

By now the Germans had used up nearly two-thirds of their ammunition and it became clear to Captain Schulze-Hinrichs that the British would fight to the last shell rather than allow his ships to break through. By 18.00 that evening he had had enough and, after receiving orders from Admiral Schmundt to abandon the fight and head south-east to find the crippled *Edinburgh*, some 200 miles away, he broke off the engagement.

Richmond's bluff had succeeded. He at once signalled *Edinburgh* that the enemy were probably heading for the cruiser, and after collecting her consorts *Bulldog* joined the convoy and set course westward for home. Later that day the commanding officer of *Beagle*, Commander Ralph Medley, signalled Commander Richmond: 'I should hate to play poker with you.'

Edinburgh, meanwhile, had made but little progress southward at her speed of only 2 knots. The crew, hungry, cold and exhausted by being at constant action stations, were also running into a debt of sleep. *Bulldog*'s signal was received with alarm by Admiral Bonham-Carter. No doubt it was only a matter of time before the enemy would find them. His only hope of defence lay with the two small destroyers *Foresight* and *Forester*, though they would be no match for the Germans. While it was true that the little group of minesweepers was speeding towards them from Murmansk, their puny armament could give little support even if they arrived in time.

At 18.00 that evening of 1 May, the Russian tug *Rubin* arrived and, after accidentally bumping the cruiser, managed to secure a tow wire to *Edinburgh* and began the task of hauling her eastward. But to no avail, for the tug proved not equal to the task. Then just before midnight the four British minesweepers *Hussar*, *Harrier*, *Gossamer* and *Niger* arrived, and with the two destroyers formed a screen around the cruiser. To the north the three German destroyers *Hermann Schoemann*, Z24 and Z25 raced through the night at 35 knots towards *Edinburgh*. There would be no difficulty in finding the cruiser for Teichert was following from a safe distance and transmitting signals. Following his humiliating withdrawal from Richmond's escorts, Schulze-Hinrichs was determined that his attack on the British cruiser would succeed.

To gain the best advantage he planned to approach *Edinburgh* from the north with his consorts in line abreast, and when within effective range they would turn and fire torpedoes simultaneously. It seemed unlikely that the crippled and unmanoeuvrable cruiser could escape from such a concentrated attack. At 06.00 on the morning of 2 May, the German force came upon a long oil slick leading south. The rest was easy. Fifteen minutes later a large shape was seen to starboard through the mist and snow and the three ships changed course. It was the prey they were seeking.

First to sight the German destroyers was the minesweeper *Hussar*. She at once opened fire with her two 4-inch guns. This was the opening phase in the memorable and heroic battle which followed in defence of *Edinburgh*. As courageously as *Bulldog* had resisted attack against overwhelming odds, so the little minesweeper accepted the challenge with a display of spirited resistance. But eventually, hopelessly outgunned and straddled by heavy shells, she had no choice but to retreat a little towards the support of the two British destroyers.

Amid the brilliant flashing of gunfire through the mist, *Edinburgh* cast off the tow wire and, in a desperate attempt to avoid being a sitting target, managed to increase her speed to 8 knots. Although the stern wreckage, acting as a rudder, kept turning her in complete circles, it was preferable to lying almost stopped.

The enemy's guns now began to find their range, falling just short of the cruiser. At the same time *Foresight* and *Forester* raced in towards the enemy with all guns blazing. In terms of fire-power the action was very much one-sided. Schulze-Hinrich's earlier attack on the convoy had been against four small British destroyers; now he was faced with only two, and these with only 4.7-inch guns. His twelve 6-inch guns gave him all the superiority in fire-power he needed.

Foresight and *Forester* sped on, turning together and firing a spread of torpedoes. Even *Edinburgh*, yawing this way and that like a wounded animal, proved she was not the sacrificial gift the Germans might have supposed. Only one of her four turrets was operational, though it had to be worked manually since all electric power had been destroyed. Each time the German destroyers crossed her line of fire the cruiser's guns flashed out. Schulze-Hinrich's plan of firing a concentrated spread of torpedoes was thrown into confusion by the attacking strategy of the two British destroyers. On the next complete circle *Edinburgh*'s single turret guns were again loaded and ready. With the director control out of action all firing had to be controlled by the young turret officer, Lieutenant R. M. Howe, who watched the battle with his head and shoulders out through the hatch at the top of the turret.

Suddenly *Hermann Schoemann* appeared out of a snow-cloud across Howe's line of fire. He immediately gave the order to fire and the cruiser's guns thundered out, spewing tongues of flame. The shells found their target in a cataclysm of fire and black smoke, smashing through the hull and bulkheads like paper. Both engine rooms were utterly destroyed, many men were killed and wounded and all control systems brought to a standstill. *Hermann Schoemann* drifted to a stop.

To some extent the tables had now been turned. For this incredible feat of gunnery Lieutenant Howe was later awarded the DSC. The original attacking posture of the enemy had now been changed into one of defence. Their main concern was to rescue as many survivors from the command ship as possible while maintaining a barrage of gunfire on the British ships. A bitter battle now developed, with *Foresight* and *Forester* exchanging fire with Z24 and Z25 in and out of the drifting snow-clouds. It was in one of these running exchanges that *Forester* was hit by five enemy shells, killing many of the crew including its commanding officer, Lieutenant-Commander Huddart.

With stricken *Forester* dead in the water and literally under the guns of the enemy, *Foresight* raced in to the defence of her sister ship and drew upon herself the full wrath of the enemy's fire. She received two direct hits which killed many of her crew, including the first lieutenant, Lieutenant-Commander Richard Fawdrey. Despite being badly damaged, she managed to raise enough power to retire slowly towards *Edinburgh* which was still circling and firing whenever the opportunity arose. *Forester*, however, was lying helpless, awaiting the *coup de grâce*, while her stokers and engineers worked frantically among the wreckage to start the engines.

It was at this moment that the crew above decks watched in horror as the tracks of two torpedoes were seen racing towards them. Frozen into inaction, they waited for the final explosion which might hurl them into eternity. But in that moment of indescribable dread, the two killer torpedoes passed under the ship and sped onward in the direction of the circling cruiser, one of them losing speed and splashing along the surface. It was this torpedo that struck the cruiser dead centre, and for the third time in as many days, *Edinburgh* lifted and shook from the impact of the great explosion. The Germans however were quite unaware of their success, engaged as they were in the violent gun battle. For *Edinburgh* it was the death blow. Despite this, her guns continued firing, her shells falling around the German ships.

By this time, *Forester* had managed to raise enough steam to get moving, and as she also retired, the eightieth round from her after gun scored a direct hit on Z25. At the same time she laid down a heavy smokescreen to shield her sister ship *Foresight* which was by now receiving the full attention of Z24.

During all these encounters the four minesweepers repeatedly dashed forward, firing their little guns and acting, as the Admiralty reported, 'like young terriers'. Remarkably, as was proved later, the minesweepers' courageous action in the mist and smoke and flame of battle gave the enemy the impression they were British destroyers arriving to support the cruiser. It was this that in all probability prevented them from launching any further attacks. In fact, with both British destroyers critically damaged and most of their guns out of action, there was nothing but the little group of minesweepers to prevent them from destroying every British ship.

In the event, with the *Hermann Schoemann* now a sinking wreck and Z25 slightly damaged, the Germans broke off the action and applied all their efforts in rescuing as many as possible from the command ship. This accomplished, they set two depth charges and scuttled the vessel. A little later the two German destroyers, packed with dejected survivors, set off across the Barents Sea for their base at Kirkenes. The enterprise which promised so much had proved not to be the unqualified success they had imagined.

In the German records of the battle an interesting and dramatic account of their own situation emerges. When their destroyers broke out of the snowcloud and came upon *Edinburgh* they found themselves much closer than they had planned. Nearest to the British ship was the command destroyer *Hermann Schoemann*, and amidst a hail of shell-fire which fell all around her she raced straight ahead. As a result of the unexpected closeness, frantic efforts were made to change the torpedo settings from long range to short. Several minutes later *Hermann Schoemann* signalled all ships to turn and fire, but at that moment Z24's and Z25's view of the cruiser was obstructed by a sudden snow squall. *Schoemann* was almost half a mile ahead at that time, and as she turned to launch torpedoes three large water spouts were seen a few yards astern, clear evidence of 6-inch shell bursts. They now knew that these must have been fired from the apparently helpless *Edinburgh*.

For a crippled ship the gunfire was remarkably accurate. Later, a salvo struck *Schoemann* with disastrous results. Both engine rooms were wiped out, all power cut and gun-control badly affected, all in one stroke. *Schoemann*'s captain, Heinrich Wittig, later recalled: 'That the cruiser should have managed to hit such vital areas of the ship was the worst possible luck that could have overtaken us.'

As *Schoemann* turned to starboard she lost way and slowly came to a halt. Smoke floats were thrown overboard in an attempt to hide the stricken ship but the British destroyers, avoiding the smokescreen, continued darting in and firing. Although fire control was destroyed, one forward gun was fired over open sights. It was then discovered that the firing mechanism of one set of torpedo tubes was jammed and the other set impacted in one position. Despite this, three torpedoes were fired as a British destroyer crossed the line of fire. The chief engineer officer Lieutenant Lorenz Bohmer, having checked the destruction below, confirmed that both engine rooms had been destroyed. Although great efforts were made to control fire outbreaks and steam escapes, those areas became untenable. It was obvious that the *Hermann Schoemann* was doomed and Wittig was forced to give the order 'Prepare to blow up the ship — destroy secret documents and take lifesaving equipment'. Despite the general damage, one of the short-wave radio transmitters was repaired allowing contact to be established with their consorts.

Renewing the bombardment of the enemy, Z24 and Z25 laid down a smokescreen to cover *Schoemann* and as the cruiser and a destroyer came on sight the commanding officer of Z25, Lieutenant-Commander Peters, fired a spread of torpedoes. It was one of these that passed under the destroyer and went on to strike *Edinburgh* the fatal blow. Z25 succeeded in severely damaging the two British destroyers by accurate gunfire from their heavier guns, then darted back to provide a further smokescreen. She also assisted her sister ship, Z24, which was trying to come alongside *Schoemann* to rescue the crew but was being subjected to shells from the enemy. These attempts proved so dangerous that the rescue was abandoned. About 07.30 Schulze-Hinrichs transmitted the message 'Calling all ships. Am abandoning ship. *Schoemann* is finished.' Immediately Z24 signalled 'Can we come alongside?', and received the reply 'Yes, but hurry'. Minutes later the nearby Z25 received a direct hit in the signals office causing severe casualties. By 08.00 Z24 managed to come alongside with her guns still firing, enabling a few men to jump across.

Soon the whole crew except for those killed and others who had managed to escape in boats and rafts were taken off. While the doomed vessel lay listing and helpless, a petty officer managed to get below and open the valves. At the same time, on the upper deck a depth charge was made ready and the time fuse set. By now the only man left on board was Lieutenant Konrad Loerke who went below and pulled the fuse of the second depth charge. Seconds later he clambered on to a life-raft and pushed off, later to be picked up by one of the boats.

Within minutes the two depth charges exploded and the big Narvik class destroyer lifted her bows and sank rapidly into the water. Unable now to renew the engagement with the British destroyers, Z24 and Z25, filled with survivors from *Schoemann*, began their withdrawals. Schulze-Hinrichs, realizing that there was no opportunity to stop and rescue the men on the rafts and in the boats, transmitted a message on all U-boat wavelengths: 'Square 5917 – save *Schoemann* survivors.' Six hours later, U-boat 88, commanded by Lieutenant Heino Bohmann, surfaced and picked up the half-dead men. It was indeed an ignominious end to a spirited but over-confident endeavour.

CHAPTER NINE

Edinburgh's Last Hours

To return to *Edinburgh*. When the stray torpedo was seen heading into the path of the circling cruiser, bridge personnel watched in dread as the lethal steel fish neared. It struck dead amidships opposite the area where the second torpedo had plunged into the ship three days earlier. This almost cut the ship in two. The huge explosion which followed ripped out the centre of the vessel and killed many more below decks. It was the end, for the cruiser shuddered to a stop and began to settle in the water. Gradually, reports from damage control informed the bridge that the ship was open from port to starboard with only the upper deck and bits of bulkhead holding her together. The situation was hopeless, and the admiral, fully aware that she might fall apart at any moment, gave the order to abandon ship. He then signalled the minesweepers to come alongside to take off the wounded, the crew and passengers.

Below decks it was a battle for survival. The explosion had ripped open oil tanks and ruptured bulkheads. Able Seaman Wallis, one of the survivors, described what happened:

It was just like being in a bad car crash. All the lights went out and we were left in darkness – a blackness that defied description. Amid the deafening roar of scalding steam erupting from burst pipes, thick fuel oil spurted in all directions from a dozen or more fractures enveloping us in its filthy black slime. In trying to breathe we found we were swallowing the stuff. In the blackness, trying to feel our way we kept losing direction. Our one hope was to find the ladder and by clearing the lockers I eventually managed to reach it.

But I had a man with a broken leg hanging around my neck and as I tried to climb the ladder he was slipping from me. The ladder was also covered in oil and I couldn't get a proper grip. I managed to hold him on to me, pulling him up and out towards a glimmer of light coming from a slit in a gangway somewhere high above. I could hear screaming from below – 'Help me – help me'. By this time my eyes were getting used to the darkness and I went down again. At the bottom of the ladder they were fighting to get up. I managed to grab one man and it turned out to be a pal of mine. Coated in black oil however you couldn't tell one man from another. By this time I had to get out because my lungs were bursting with the smell and having swallowed some I was vomiting. After a few minutes I went down to the hatch again to see if I could do anything, only to discover that the heavy cover had fallen down with the listing and had jammed shut. I got some help but although we tried, we couldn't move it. They were still screaming when we left. I remember hearing the hoarse cries of one man in particular. He was from our mess, a real tough guy and a bully; everybody was afraid of him, he made life a misery. He had no regard for man, no respect for God. But at that moment, facing eternity, he became a gibbering infant, screaming and crying for the Lord to help him. He died with the rest down there. But we had to go, as the list was increasing. Up on deck we found that one of the minesweepers had come alongside and was already taking the wounded and passengers aboard. While we waited our turn, we huddled together behind the hangar out of the freezing wind. We were all in pretty bad shape and I went across to the wardroom to find a cloth to wipe the oil from our eyes.

There was a door open near the wardroom leading into the Major of Marine's cabin. On the bed lay a clean white sheet and pulling it away I ripped it up for some of the others to have a piece each. My shoes at the time were squelching with oil and seeing a pair of tapered shoes sticking out under the bunk, I grabbed them and put them on and wore them all the time I was in Russia. I went back to wipe my pal's eyes and the back of his neck and as I did so the flesh came off with the oil. He must have caught the full force of one of the steam bursts.

One of the radar ratings, Harry Cook, had a miraculous escape:

There were eight of us in this lower compartment when the torpedo hit. The deck plating above us, yielding under the force of the explosion jammed the hatch cover. In charge of us was a long-term petty officer who treated us with contempt. He despised us not only because we were young and inexperienced but principally because we were 'hostilities only'. We all shouted and battered at the hatch but no one heard us. Eventually, by exerting all our combined strength against the cover, we managed to move it open just wide enough to allow the petty officer to force his body through the gap and slide out. We were all very young and very frightened and the tension was terrible. We waited there in the dark for nearly an hour assuring ourselves that the P.O. would soon be bringing help. But still no-one came. We tried the telephone but could get no reply. After what seemed an eternity the phone actually rang. It was from Damage Control. The voice said – 'We didn't know you were down there, we thought you were all out. We saw the Petty Officer who came barging up the ladder and when we asked – "Is everybody out?", he replied "Yes". As a result we locked the upper hatch cover in the deck above.' Very soon a Damage Control party arrived and forced the cover open and in moments we were free. You can imagine how we felt. In fact if we could have found that P.O. at the time, I think we would have half killed him. By his deliberate neglect we could have all died.

The withdrawal of the German forces came as a great relief to Captain Faulkner, for as he later reported, 'I shall never understand why they didn't come in and finish us off. I think they acknowledged defeat after being so heavily shot at.'

The minesweepers *Harrier* and *Gossamer* secured alongside the slowly sinking cruiser and the loading of wounded and passengers began. With the ship listing heavily and the decks of the two ships at different heights in the lifting swell, it was not an easy task. Accidents among the stretcher cases were common. Some fell off the stretchers and crashed on to the decks of the rescuing ships. Others, naked from their sick beds, unsure of their footing, fell over the side to become entangled in the safety nets, nearly freezing to death in the bitter Arctic wind. Salvaging of the mass of gold bullion deep in the bomb room, now covered in tons of sea water, was out of the question. Precious lives were at stake and time was of the essence. The cruiser could break apart at any moment.

Finally Admiral Bonham-Carter and Captain Faulkner clambered off the cruiser for the last time. Everyone had acted with courage and fortitude in this dangerous situation. Later, Captain Faulkner said of the ordeal, 'Emergencies were met with such calmness and confidence they ceased to be emergencies.' The two minesweepers pulled away from *Edinburgh* and the other escorts stood off to watch the cruiser go down.

Yet even in these last moments she seemed reluctant to die, and *Foresight* was ordered to fire her one remaining torpedo. The missile plunged far into the bowels of the cruiser with a booming explosion. Slowly, like a dying creature, the great cruiser rolled over on to her side. As the bows rose high so the stern disappeared below the surface. All that remained was the stench of fuel oil drifting over the freezing water.

As *Edinburgh* sank beneath the waves, carrying down the bodies of all those killed aboard her, not far away the *Hermann Schoemann* was settling on the ocean bed with her dead. For both sides there had been neither victory nor defeat, and both had suffered the loss of an important ship. *Harrier*'s log recorded that *Edinburgh* sank in position 71.51° north, 35.10° east, at 09.00, 2 May 1942.

An hour later, as the cold Arctic wind whistled over the waters above *Edinburgh*'s resting-place, with no ship visible from one horizon to another, the black dripping hull of U456 surfaced near the floating wreckage. From the conning tower hatch emerged the man responsible for the destruction of the British cruiser, Lieutenant Max Teichert. In Norway, the German High Command was still unaware that *Edinburgh* had been sunk. Teichert was now able to provide confirmation. While the gun and torpedo battle had raged on the surface, the submerged U456 had positioned herself close to the cruiser but at a depth of forty feet to avoid danger. At 09.00 Teichert heard the familiar sounds of a large ship sinking. He later reported: 'She was so near, we were all afraid she would fall on top of us.'

But now as he studied the sea around him there was no doubt that the cruiser had sunk. A great oil slick covered the area and within it a mass of floating caps, uniforms, tables and papers. With a sense of deep satisfaction he descended into the submarine and set course for Norway, knowing he could claim a major success in this pitiless war between Germany and the Allies. Some miles to the south, the little group of British ships with their survivors headed for the safety of the Kola inlet, and the following morning those who were fit were landed at Polyarnoe and Vaenga, while the wounded were taken to Murmansk.

On his arrival at Murmansk, *Harrier*'s commanding officer Captain Hinton was handed the following letter, quoted verbatim, from the captain of the Russian tug *Rubin* which had accidentally rammed *Edinburgh* on its approach:

Dear Sir,
Soviet's seaman was witness of heroic battle of English seamen with predominants powers of enemy. English seamen did observe their sacred duty before Fatherland. We are prouding to staunchness and courage of English seamens – our Allies. I am very sorry what injured your ship by approach to board for what I must to beg pardon.

Commander of Division

It was a letter that was greatly appreciated by everyone. Later, at Murmansk, Admiral Bonham-Carter despatched the following message to the captain and crew of *Harrier*:

. . . it was inspiring to see the minesweepers on the scene of action and taking every opportunity of firing at the enemy when visibility permitted. The manner in which *Harrier* and *Gossamer* were brought alongside the listing *Edinburgh* during the action showed a fine feat of seamanship and I fully confirm the Commanding Officer of *Edinburgh*'s report of the way we were treated on board. Never have I seen more kindness and attention than was given to myself, Captain, officers and men than by the Captain, officers and ship's company of *Harrier*.

He also sent the following report to the commander-in-chief of the home fleet, Admiral Sir John Tovey.

When the third torpedo hit *Edinburgh* on the port side just before the catapult and practically opposite the place where the first torpedo had struck on the starboard side, I realized that the ship must be open from side to side and this was later confirmed by reports from below. I considered that she might break in two at any moment and sink and as the ship was slowly settling, I instructed the Captain to 'abandon ship'. It was with great reluctance that the order was given entirely on my own responsibility. I felt it was quite impossible to save her. I have since spent many hours thinking over this decision and am still convinced that it was the only possible step to take and if placed in the same position again I should give the same order. Had I kept men on board any longer many valuable lives would certainly have been lost. I cannot understand the behaviour of the German destroyers unless as stated in the report of the Senior Officer of the 6th Minesweeper Flotilla, they mistook the minesweepers for destroyers and did not realize the condition *Edinburgh* was in. If they had shown any real determination I consider that not only *Edinburgh* but possibly all ships present could have been sunk. When *Edinburgh* was finally abandoned there were not many enemy ships in sight and although gunfire was heard later after I embarked in *Harrier* they were not seen again. It is probable therefore they were not aware that the ship was actually sunk and it is possible they did not realize that one of their torpedoes had hit.

I cannot speak too highly of the behaviour of the Captain, officers and men of *Edinburgh* from the time she was first torpedoed. The coolness, calmness and cheerfulness shown by the Captain was felt right through the ship and at no time was there any sign of depression through the intense cold and lack

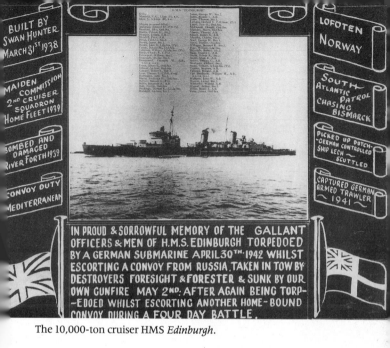

The 10,000-ton cruiser HMS *Edinburgh*.

HMS *Trinidad* bombed, on fire and sinking, May 1942.

HMS *Edinburgh*'s quarterdeck after torpedo hits. Sunk May 1942.

The 8,000-ton cruiser HMS *Trinidad* leaving Devonport, October 1941.

The 12,000-ton German pocket battleship, *Lutzow*.

The German destroyer *Eckholdt*, sunk December 1942.

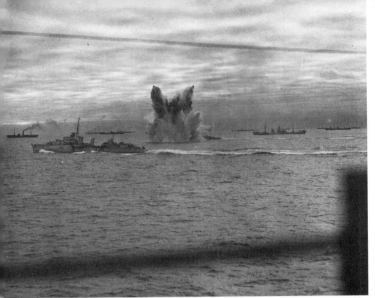

Bomb falling between HMS *Eskimo* and HMS *Wheatland*. Convoy
P Q 18, September 1942.

The 14,000-ton German heavy cruiser *Admiral Hipper* in Altenfiord.

First Sea Lord, Admiral of the Fleet Sir Dudley Pound GCB, OM, GCVO, KCB, CB.

Captain Robert St Vincent Sherbrooke VC, RN.

Grand Admiral Carl Donitz, Commander-in-Chief, German Navy, from January 1943.

Grand Admiral Erich Raeder, Commander-in-Chief, German Navy, resigned January 1943.

The 32,000-ton German battlecruiser *Scharnhorst*, sunk in the Arctic, December 1943.

Conditions on the fo'c'sle in Arctic waters.

The mighty German battleship *Tirpitz* of 43,000 tons.

The capsized *Tirpitz* after suffering hits from three 12,000-lb bombs, November 1944.

Law Society Union, Plymouth Hoe, May 1969.

of sleep nor loss of heart despite the knowledge that surface, submarine and air attack was imminent.

The way in which *Foresight* and *Forester* went into attack superior forces and the manner in which they were handled could not have been more gallant.

I would like to place on record my deep appreciation for all that has been done for us by the Senior British Naval Officer at Murmansk and his staff under the most difficult circumstances with inadequate facilities. Over 1000 survivors from *Edinburgh* and other ships have been housed, fed and where necessary clothed and their individual kindness will never be forgotten. It is no doubt fully realized how deeply I regret the loss of so fine a cruiser but I hope it will be appreciated that I alone was responsible for the movement of *Edinburgh* and that in no way can any criticism be levelled at Captain Faulkner who I hope will be given another sea command as early as possible.

Rear-Admiral commanding 18th Cruiser Squadron,
Rear-Admiral Stuart Bonham-Carter.

The *Edinburgh* survivors who were put ashore at Vaenga and Polyarnoe, while thankful to be alive, viewed their prospects with some despondency. They had been under the impression that in a few days they would be embarking on ships bound for home. But this was not to be, and in the weeks and months that followed they were to undergo much discomfort, hunger, cold and many other privations before returning home. Sadly, many were to perish in attempts to reach the United Kingdom.

The loss of the bullion had its sequel nearly forty years later when a successful attempt was made to recover the gold from the ocean floor. During the latter part of August 1981, the 1400-ton salvage vessel *Stephaniturm,* owned by Jessop Marine Ltd, located the cruiser at a depth of 800 feet using remote robot cameras. *Stephaniturm,* one of the world's most advanced diving vessels, is so designed that a diving bell can be suspended from a chamber within her hull. From it a diver, wearing a special suit through which hot water circulated to combat the intense cold, swam down to the wreck and took a first look at the torpedo hole leading to the bomb room which contained the gold bullion. He found, however, that so much silt had penetrated over the years that it would be difficult to reach the treasure. A new access was therefore made through an empty oil fuel tank adjacent to the gold room, and divers successfully entered the compartment and began to remove the silt and wreckage covering the gold. This proved to be a highly delicate and dangerous operation as all around lay explosives scattered by the torpedo blast which had sunk *Edinburgh* in May 1942. On 16 September, in great excitement, diver John Rossier informed the diving supervisor over the intercom that he had located one of the gold ingots. Eventually a total of £45 million-worth of gold ingots was recovered, of which about £20 million went to Jessop Marine. Of the remainder the Russians, whose gold it was in the first place, took two-thirds, and the British government one-third.

Bared of her gold, *Edinburgh* now lies in the calm darkness and peace of her grave, alone with her memories of a heroic past.

CHAPTER TEN

The Barents Sea Claims Another Cruiser

By the spring of 1942 the sea war was speeding to a climax, with the Allies reeling under losses they could ill afford and gaining few successes. Britain had lost three of her best battleships, *Prince of Wales*, *Repulse* and *Hood*. In the Arctic and Atlantic oceans, German submarines were gaining the upper hand. Production of U-boats had been increased and they were being launched at the incredible rate of five a week. There were now over 100 submarines along the convoy routes, capable of sinking thousands of tons of Allied shipping. Despite some Allied successes the balance was in favour of the Germans, and much was to happen before the tide turned.

The steel plates brought by *Edinburgh* to repair the enormous damage suffered by the cruiser HMS *Trinidad*, now in dry dock at Vaenga, were soon put to good use. Russian women welders were employed to fasten the plates into position and to build supports out of massive timbers. The Russians had no steel girders to spare as every bit of metal was needed for their own defensive positions in the front line. The finished repairs were at best only a patched-up job. Timber supports were not a satisfactory answer to the strain that would be put upon them in the Arctic storms that would have to be faced on the return voyage, but it was the best that could be done with the materials available.

By 12 May *Trinidad* was as ready to sail as she could be under the circumstances. That day she took aboard sixty *Edinburgh* survivors and an equal number of merchant navy survivors of various nationalities from crippled ships of earlier convoys. Just before midnight on the 13th the cruiser left the Kola inlet with the intention of reaching Philadelphia, USA, for permanent repairs and a refit. The sailing of any ship on the 13th is interpreted as a bad omen by sailors the world over. This was no exception. Men openly expressed their fears that the voyage would end in tragedy. Just prior to the sailing, Admiral Bonham-Carter transferred his flag to *Trinidad*, and as the Russian coast faded from view he and Captain Saunders searched the horizon for the promised Russian support planes. They had been given a firm assurance of fighter protection for the first 250 miles. Three aircraft eventually appeared but remained for barely forty-five minutes before returning to their base at Vaenga.

Hardly had they disappeared than a German Condor reconnaissance plane arrived on the horizon, sending signals to base at Petsamo and Kirkenes giving the course and position of the cruiser. *Trinidad* had four escort destroyers, the battle-damaged *Foresight* and *Forester*, and the *Somali* and *Matchless*. So much damage had been suffered by the two destroyers that had defended *Edinburgh* a fortnight earlier that it was literally a case of the crippled aiding the crippled.

At midday on the 14th *Trinidad* found her northward course barred by the appearance of the ice barrier, so she altered course westward. At the same time U-boats were spotted and it was obvious that all submarines in the area had been alerted. During that afternoon a stream of signals was received on the bridge confirming that the Germans were preparing to strike.

This was indeed true, for in north Norway tactical plans were being drawn up at Banak and Bardufoss to launch a full-scale attack on the cruiser. Last-minute orders were given by Major Blodorn operating the Junker 88 dive-bombing squadron and Colonel Roth commanding the Heinkel 111 torpedo group. The young pilots were part of a crack Luftwaffe squadron brought in from Italy to strengthen the Norway groups to ensure the destruction of every Allied convoy that tried to run the gauntlet across the Barents Sea between North Cape and Bear Island. As the hours passed, more shadowing aircraft and more U-boats arrived. The vultures were gathering.

Whereas in March *Trinidad* had been able to take refuge from dive-bombers in the snow squalls, now there was no fog, no snow, little cloud and not even a sea mist. Such clouds as there were would favour the dive-bombers for they were light and misty, providing cover high above the sea. There would be no hours of darkness either for at this time of year there were twenty-four hours of daylight.

At nine o'clock that evening the radar operators reported formations of aircraft approaching. Reports to the bridge became more frequent: 'A wave of aircraft at 15 miles' – 'Another at 30 miles' – 'There are more coming in at 40 miles' – 'Another at 60 miles' – , and then from the radar room – 'The screen is full of aircraft, sir.'

Then came the insistent clamour of alarm bells and with it the heart-stopping announcement – 'Action stations – action. Prepare to repel enemy aircraft.' Within

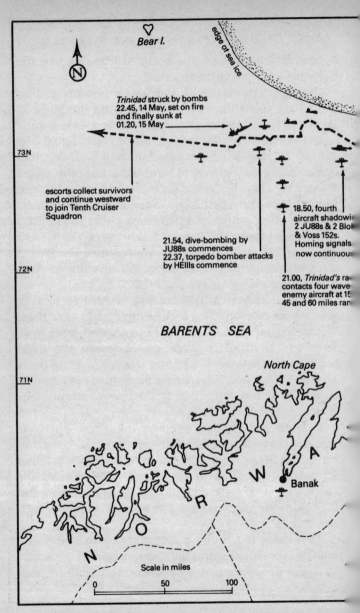

Bear I.

edge of sea ice

Trinidad struck by bombs
22.45, 14 May, set on fire
and finally sunk at
01.20, 15 May

73N

escorts collect survivors
and continue westward
to join Tenth Cruiser
Squadron

18.50, fourth
aircraft shadowi
2 JU88s & 2 Blo
& Voss 152s.
Homing signals
now continuou

21.54, dive-bombing by
JU88s commences
22.37, torpedo bomber attacks
by HEIIIs commence

21.00, *Trinidad's* ra
contacts four wave
enemy aircraft at 1
45 and 60 miles ran

72N

BARENTS SEA

North Cape

71N

Banak

Scale in miles

0   50   100

The Sinking of *HMS Trinidad*, 15 May 1942

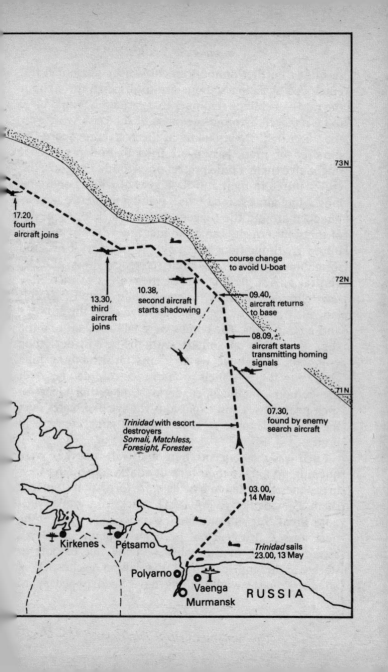

73N

17.20,
fourth
aircraft joins

course change
to avoid U-boat

72N

13.30,
third
aircraft
joins

10.38,
second aircraft
starts shadowing

09.40,
aircraft returns
to base

08.09,
aircraft starts
transmitting homing
signals

71N

07.30,
found by enemy
search aircraft

Trinidad with escort
destroyers
*Somali, Matchless,
Foresight, Forester*

03.00,
14 May

Trinidad sails
23.00, 13 May

Kirkenes   Petsamo

Polyarno

Vaenga

Murmansk   RUSSIA

seconds a further announcement – 'Key personnel not employed at action stations are to disperse throughout the ship' – a chilling reminder that casualties would have to be replaced by other members of the crew whenever they occurred. Down below in the recreation space the hundred or more passengers tried to find places that might give them a little protection. Around the guns, the crews attired in their anti-flash gear of white hoods and long white gloves stood tense, waiting in silence, fingers wrapped around the triggers. Then, just before ten, out of the southern sky came the first low whisper merging into a rhythmic hum like a swarm of angry bees, and formations of Junker 88s came screaming down at near-vertical angles, pulling out of their dives at incredibly low altitudes as they released their bombs. Simultaneously came the deafening barrage of all the cruiser's anti-aircraft guns. The bombs were falling all around the ship, exploding on contact with the sea in deafening eruptions, with huge water-spouts mushrooming high above the ship's funnels to fall in ice-cold deluges over the gunners on the open decks. Under the impact of such near misses and explosions the welded plates over the ruptured torpedo hole strained and creaked in protest.

Such was the concentration of aircraft that they were queuing up to take their turn to attack. Expending their loads, they returned to base as more formations replaced them. For nearly two hours the attacks continued without a break, the ship shuddering under the impact of the near misses. If it had not been for Captain Saunders's astute handling of the ship, swinging her to port or starboard in anticipation of the fall of each stick of bombs, *Trinidad* would surely have been ripped apart.

After each order the ship swung away, agonizingly slowly, from the line of falling bombs, barely avoiding them. The four escorting destroyers were also receiving their share of the attack but the main concentration was upon *Trinidad*. Captain Saunders's main concern was with the welded plates. Even if the ship came through without a direct hit, just how long could the plates take the battering from the near misses?

But now a new emergency arose. While the gunners had their hands full fighting off the planes overhead, the torpedo bombers arrived. They appeared as little dots at first, low on the horizon – Heinkel 115s and 111s, each carrying two torpedoes. Skimming just above the water, they came in line ahead in a wide circle. Sections of the already exhausted gun crews were now switched on to these new targets, which meant depressing the 4-inch guns until they were firing downwards at the oncoming aircraft. Whatever plan of action this new enemy had in mind, it was rudely shattered by the intensity of the counter barrage laid down. The whole line of aircraft turned away, showing they had no liking for the shells bursting among them. Minutes later they returned in line abreast, approaching from the quarter and beam. Again the fire-power proved too fearsome and once more they turned away.

Already twice frustrated, they now approached in two groups, one on the port and the other on the starboard quarter, releasing their torpedoes at surface level. Fortunately the tracks could be clearly seen and *Trinidad* was able to swing clear of the trails in time to see the deadly tin fish go speeding by on either side. During this surge of activity, the overhead bombers pressed home their attack in a cleverly concerted movement with the torpedo bombers. Gathering for the kill as though determined to deliver the death blow, the Heinkels again circled and came in for a further assault, launching their torpedoes well within the dropping zone. At the same time, one of the Junkers attacking from cloud cover immediately overhead came roaring down, releasing its load of four bombs at barely 400 feet. The situation was fraught with peril – bombs or torpedoes.

Cruisers cannot be made to turn and dodge about as easily as little motor boats. *Trinidad* was in the middle of a turn to port to avoid three torpedoes heading straight for her but this was putting her directly into the line of the falling bombs. The outcome was inevitable. The four 500-pound missiles were dead on target, falling straight on the bridge superstructure. The impact was terrifying, a miniature earthquake blinding the senses. Damage to the ship was disastrous. One bomb landed just a few feet in front of the bridge between the parapet and B turret, boring its way through the admiral's sea cabin, through the Fleet Air Arm office and the canteen and exploding in the stokers' and petty officers' mess deck. The blast went upwards, hurling the bridge personnel into the sides of the bridge structure, blowing away the port side of B gun deck and forming a huge crater in the fo'c'sle deck.

In minutes the crater was ablaze, with fire spreading rapidly to other mess decks. Another bomb skimmed along the side of the ship and exploded just under the waterline, tearing off the temporarily welded plates like paper, allowing tons of water to flood in on all those ratings who were battened down at their action stations, and creating a list to starboard. The other two bombs grazed down the port side, exploding abreast of the fo'c'sle, fracturing the forward compartments and causing them to flood. The Junker that had caused the damage was blasted by a stream of pom-pom shells as it tried to escape and it plunged into the sea.

The crater was now a cauldron of fire, creeping aft below the bridge structure and destroying the water mains necessary for fire-fighting. The flames were also getting uncomfortably close to the forward magazines containing cordite and shells. Captain Saunders now had an agonizing decision to make. Already more torpedo bombers were forming for an attack. If he stopped the ship to prevent the wind fanning the flames, the cruiser would be an easy target for the enemy. If on the other hand the ship was kept going to dodge the torpedoes the fire might reach unmanageable proportions. He took the latter course, as there was always the chance that the fires could be controlled, whereas there was little possibility of the ship recovering from further torpedo hits.

The canteen and recreation spaces, filled with returning passengers, were only a few feet from the place where one of the 500-pound bombs exploded. Few, if any, of the men in these sections survived. Assistant canteen manager Jack Holman, whose action station was close to the chief and petty officers' mess, had a miraculous escape:

> When the bomb exploded in the near compartment, there was a massive yellow flash. I was hurled forward, hitting the bulkhead and losing consciousness. When I recovered, blood was pouring from a gash on my forehead and a split under the eye. In fact my eyes were so filled with blood that I thought

at first I was blind. The ship was listing over at such an angle that I had to crawl downwards towards the ship's side and from there I stumbled along, blindly feeling my way, climbing over and through the twisted girders and bulkheads which had been torn from the decking. My physical condition was bad enough but the situation was aggravated by the darkness and the volume of smoke pouring up from somewhere below, enveloping me like a blanket. How I found the ladder leading to the upper deck I'll never know. Coughing and gasping for breath I managed to make it to the top, feeling the cold fresh air on my face. Suddenly, strong arms were reaching down and pulling me upwards and outwards on to the deck. I must have been the last man out from the area below, the last of only eight in my little section, for the Canteen and Recreation Space in which the passengers had been accommodated had been utterly destroyed. It was in this same area a damage control party was completely wiped out. Just before the bombs fell, a few radar operators were on the flag deck watching the falling bombs and frequently taking cover from shrapnel. They realized it was only a matter of time before hits would be scored. Jim Harper and three others decided it would be safer to go below.

It was as they neared the canteen flat that the bomb exploded immediately ahead of them. Jim Harper relates:

I lay on the deck, at the foot of the ladder leading to the bridge. I heard the first bomb go off somewhere nearby and a moment later, another seemed to explode about twenty feet away, throwing debris over my head. With all this, I was aware of something tearing down through the bridge structure and steel decking, like a machine crashing through plywood. I covered my face with my arms, as a grey shape shot through the deck in front of me, a blinding sheet of flame enveloping me as the iron rivets burst from the deck on which I lay. I was aware of being lifted into the air, with the deck curling round me like paper. Later I came to – how much later I don't know. It seemed very quiet; then high above me, there was the tinkle of a small piece of metal falling. Suddenly I realized the air was hot, in fact the deck and bulkheads which my groping hands were touching were growing hotter every minute. Through the dense billowing smoke pouring out from somewhere just ahead, I noticed the dull glow of fire. With my senses clearing, I realized I had to get out and get out quickly. I remember stepping through a hole in a bulkhead and eventually finding myself in the hangar space and staggering out on to the catapult deck, to feel the ice cold air hitting me in the face. I was pretty shaken up but still alive and in one piece. I learned later that my three mess-mates who had come below with me were blown to pieces.

Replacement damage control and rescue parties, arriving on B gun deck, found a scene of utter destruction. Besides the huge crater in the deck, the massive gun turret had been pushed over at a crazy angle, like a smashed toy, part of the ship's side had disappeared. From within the crater there were cries for help and men hurriedly lowered ropes.

Eventually five men were hauled out. The damage had reached down as far as the transmitter room and it was here that seaman Johnny Cutler found himself as he recovered consciousness covered in blood from the bodies of two other seamen lying on top of him. The shock waves from the four bombs had distorted the ship enough to jam several escape hatches. A vivid description of this problem was given by Wardroom Steward Howard Stephens, whose action station was in one of the magazines deep in the ship:

In these compartments, well below the waterline, any noise in the sea around is greatly amplified by the water. The explosions of the bombs from the near misses along the side of the ship was indeed terrifying. Suddenly there was one great explosion and I was knocked unconscious. When I recovered, I found I was lying under a pile of cordite cases, for the heavy timbers supporting the racks had snapped. I climbed the ladder and tried to get out but found the hatch had jammed. I don't think I shall ever forget the dread and dismay that came over me in those awful moments when I realized that I was trapped in this steel cell and within a ship which was probably sinking. Trying to control the panic which I felt building up inside me, I tore at the catches of the hatch but they were immovable. I recall picking up a small iron bar and banging violently on the metal roof and then shouting at the top of my voice until my throat could take no more. I could hear the shells rolling about on the deck in the shell room above me and had practically given up hope when I heard footsteps – somewhere above me. The reborn hope gave me new energy to wield my bar and shout. Suddenly there was an answering call, some banging at the hatch and the catches began to turn.

Within minutes, the cover was back and I was out and free into the shell room. My rescuer was able to tell me that he had come back to secure the shells from rolling about. However, as we were talking, the increasing list of the ship brought down a whole rack of six-inch shells, barely missing us. But by now, the hatch out of the shell room had also become jammed. There was however a possible way of escape through a small opening in which the shell hoist operated. Shirts off, we squeezed our sweating bodies through the tiny opening and we were free. The deck on the port side was a blazing inferno, with spouting debris erupting from a large crater in the deck, like a firework display.

The starboard recreation space below the bridge had two exits. One of these led to the fo'c'sle itself, the other down a hatch to emerge somewhere near the hangar. Leading Telegraphist Ron Bennett had decided to take up a position here, as he felt it would be reasonably safe. He could hear the air defence officer's running commentary describing the air attacks from a nearby speaker. He could also hear the orders being given to the anti-aircraft gunners. Suddenly the frantic call came over the speakers for the starboard pom-poms. The bombs came hurtling down, penetrated the superstructure and exploded somewhere beneath him.

As he regained consciousness he was aware that his face was stinging and that his left jaw felt extremely painful. The room seemed to have gone much darker, with clouds of smoke pouring through an open hatch-way. In the semi-conscious state he was in he managed to get his legs to respond to what his brain was urging him to do – get away as quickly as possible. He realized that his feet and ankles were giving him much pain. Slowly he managed to crawl on hands and knees through the weather door out on to the deck. It was then that he saw where the bomb had struck. A chasm had been made in the deck in front of him and, looking down, he could see a fierce fire raging. Still on hands and knees he found there was sufficient room to skirt the edges of this chasm and he was able to crawl down the starboard side towards the stern and safety. As he crawled aft, he became aware of a broken pipe somewhere up on the bridge structure which was sending down a deluge of water right in his path. Curiously enough, despite the pain he was in, his reaction was one of annoyance: 'Hell, I'm going to get wet.' But he went on and was soon spotted by others of the crew, who carried him aft to where first aid was being given.

Although he did not know it at the time, his face and hands had been badly burned. In addition, his jaw and both ankles had been fractured and lacerated, and his left eardrum destroyed. After a quick examination by the ship's doctor, who himself had a broken arm and head wounds, his face was bandaged and he was given a shot of morphine in his arm. Later he was transferred to *Foresight* where he was laid out on a mess table and attended to by a surgeon lieutenant. He had not been labelled as having been injected with morphine, with the result that he received a second dose which put him out for a very long time.

Inside B turret the force of the explosion was such that equipment was wrenched from its moorings. Captain Griffiths, who was in charge, ordered one of his marines to shout down to the magazine crews and tell them to come up, but there was no reply and when he and Sergeant Feltham listened at the hatch all that could be heard was water cascading into the compartment. Constructor Lieutenant Chatter, with the assistance of a stoker, managed to penetrate as far forward as the engine room artificers' mess, where they could hear men shouting for help. They attached a hose to the fire main but there was no pressure so they sent for protective clothing to put on before trying to once again penetrate the smoke. The heat was too great, however, and they had to abandon the attempt. The fire in the hangar had by now heated the deck above to such a degree that the small arms ammunition was igniting. Pom-pom rounds started exploding everywhere, putting up a lethal firework display.

Although *Trinidad* had been mortally hit she was fighting on. The torpedo bombers were gathering once more to attack, and five minutes later they came in low, just skimming the surface to release their torpedoes. Once again, the bright pointers of the tracer shells from the smaller guns gave excellent direction to the 4-inch guns. But though the Heinkels succeeded in dropping their deadly tin fish none found their mark.

In the meantime the bridge had been receiving more and more discouraging reports from damage control parties tackling the flooding and fires. The ship was still listing heavily to starboard and fires were spreading rapidly through the mess decks as well as in the hangars and upwards. Further down the situation was just as bad. The flames had reached the repair work that had been carried out at Vaenga, and the timber shores and oil fuel leakages were igniting and adding to the already well-established conflagration. By 23.30 the enemy attacks had abated, and Captain Saunders was able to moderate the fanning of the flames by reducing speed to 12 knots. But by now even this was too late to do much good.

At midnight, with the sun still above the horizon, the fires raged out of control. Down below near the explosion area those who remained alive, dazed and wounded, were trying to grope their way past flames and through choking smoke to safety. Below them compartments with men in them were sealed off by the flames. The bridge itself was becoming untenable as the superstructure was becoming a chimney for the fire below. The flames were roaring up the bridge companionways and ladder openings.

The state of the ship was so grave, and further attacks inevitable, that the Captain decided to abandon ship. The engines were stopped, and a broadcast was made throughout the ship. Commander Collett made the announcement, instructing everyone to muster on the quarter-deck in their respective divisions and warning them not to go back into the ship to collect their personal belongings. On the emergency bridge the admiral and the captain broadcast for Commander Skinner, the constructor. He arrived, blackened with smoke. The admiral said, 'We have ordered abandon ship, were we right?' to which Skinner replied, 'Sir, it would take the whole Glasgow fire brigade to put out this fire.'

Deep down in the telephone exchange, below the

stokers' mess deck, Coder Nicholls, recovering consciousness from the explosions, found himself alone and in
darkness. The deck above had been blown away and the
ladder with it. On hands and knees he discovered that
his two companions had been killed in the blast. No one
seemed to hear his shouts. With stoic resignation he sat
down and lit a cigarette. It was this that saved his life, for
at that very moment a stoker, running through a compartment two decks above, looked down and saw the
flare of the match. Ropes were lowered and soon Nicholls
was pulled to safety.

The destroyer *Matchless* was the first to arrive. She
nosed in carefully with great skill and due regard for the
exploding ammunition and the flames roaring around
the bridge. The stretcher cases were first loaded on to
her decks, followed by the many wounded who were
able to get aboard with assistance from willing helpers.
On the bridge of *Trinidad* Captain Saunders turned to the
officers, signalmen and messengers and said: 'It's time
we got out of here before we are burned alive.' The
present author was among those who were thankful to
clamber down the escape ladder. The other three
destroyers in the meantime circled round, providing a
screen to keep the U-boats at bay. Here and there in the
sky there were still wisps of smoke from bursting shells,
hanging like cotton wool, and the occasional column of
water rising up in the sea from falling bombs.

Radio Mechanic John Evans arrived on the quarter-
deck and was approached by an officer who asked him if
he could spare any clothing to help cover one of the
wounded waiting to be transferred. He was wearing no
coat, but freezing as he was he took off his overalls,
covered the wounded man and with three others made

up a stretcher party. This team managed to carry two more men to the ship's side but it was pretty heavy going as the ship's list was increasing. One of the men they carried was a coloured seaman who remained very cheerful even though his heels had been blown off. In the middle of this dramatic episode a man in a sorry condition appeared. He seemed to be blind and not to know what was happening to him. With compassion and great difficulty they eventually managed to lift, push and pull him over the side on to the decks of the destroyer. Only then did they discover that he hadn't been wounded at all. The man was extremely short-sighted and had lost his glasses.

Evans, still dressed only in shirt and trousers, was climbing over the rails on to the last destroyer to come alongside when another rating came along *Trinidad*'s deck. Although the ship was burning fiercely and sinking slowly under him, he found time to shout across, 'Can I interest you in a new line of gent's natty overcoats?' and threw one over to Evans.

A little earlier Shipwright Bert Soper had decided to go below to collect another coat. On the way he passed his friend 'Blackie' Cass lying down in one of the gangways wrapped in a duffel coat. He said, 'What the hell are you doing down here?' to which Cass replied, 'I decided to get some sleep.' Soper hauled him to his feet with, 'What? Go to sleep with the bloody ship sinking? Get up top.' Passing through the fire area on the way to the upper deck, they were transfixed by the sight of a seaman trapped in a light steel bulkhead which had been tightly wrapped round him by the force of the explosion. As the flames roared nearer he was screaming his way to death, but nothing could be done to extricate him as every fire main was out of action.

At this point a special tribute must be paid to a very gallant gentleman, Engineer Lieutenant J. G. Boddy. Many of his stokers were trapped below and could be heard shouting for help. This tall, very young officer stepped through a hatchway to the decks below with the remark, 'Can't leave my men below, must try to get them out.' But that part of the ship was by now an inferno. The ladder had gone and the rope he used to lower himself must have burnt through. Although a search party was organized, it was driven back by the heat. Lieutenant Boddy and the men he tried to rescue must have perished. He had been married just a week or two before *Trinidad* left Devonport. Later in the war he was posthumously awarded the Albert Medal, later renamed the George Cross.

Just as *Forester* and *Foresight* were pulling alongside the quarter-deck one of the circling torpedo bombers chose to come in on the port quarter. Up on the 4-inch gun deck Commissioned Gunner Dicky Bunt and Gunner Charles Norsworthy were covering the remaining survivors as they climbed aboard the destroyers. Dicky Bunt, running between the port and starboard sides of the gun deck, spotted the oncoming plane. With a shout of 'Nosser, there's one bastard coming in over there,' they both jumped onto the gun mounting and watched the aircraft through binoculars. The fast-approaching plane was only a mile away and about twenty feet above sea level. All the gun's electrical circuits had been destroyed, so the gunners were reduced to the primitive method of manual control, firing over open sights. With both barrels loaded they waited. The cruiser's list to starboard created difficulties when they tried to depress the guns to pick up the target, and Dicky Bunt, peering through binoculars, was shouting, 'Train left – train left – stop – up a bit – train right . . .' Changing to look through the open sight, Norsworthy lowered the guns a little to give him a target sighting between the sea and the bottom of the plane, then he fired both barrels. It was a masterful effort, for both shells burst under the plane's port wing, lifting it with such a jerk that it almost capsized. A great cheer went up from the watchers. As the shell burst the plane's torpedo fell away at a crazy angle, while smoke and flame poured out of the fuselage. Turning sharply away to starboard, the Heinkel lost height and disappeared into the sea.

These were the last shells to be fired from *Trinidad*. With the ever-increasing list to starboard, the last few survivors were having difficulty in finding a footing on the sloping decks. Several acted as anchor men by attaching themselves to the guard-rail on the higher side. From each of these several men hung, climbing together in a human chain to prevent others falling into the lower scuppers, now awash. On deck at the extremity of these chains was Commander Collett, directing each man in turn to let go and slide to the lower rail before clambering up on to the decks of *Somali*.

Able Seamen Charles Ideson and Jim Harper were among the last to make this difficult and awkward climb. As their feet touched the deck they turned to help those following and reached down to haul up a rather short, chubby man who was a stranger to them, followed by Commander Collett and, a moment later, by the last man to leave the ship – Captain Saunders.

The four destroyers stood off to watch the last

moments of the cruiser. The canting deck and settling bows clearly revealed the condition of the sinking ship. Profiled against a bank of rolling clouds of black smoke, tongues of flame from the forward turrets to the catapult deck amidships were ravaging the bridge and superstructure. The fire must have reached the after boiler room, for great clouds of smoke could be seen pouring from the after funnel as well, the huge reeking mass rising high into the sky and rolling away over the grey Barents Sea towards the red midnight sun.

To hasten her end, Admiral Bonham-Carter on *Somali* gave the painful order to *Matchless* to sink *Trinidad* with torpedoes. The crew and survivors watched the tubes being trained on the burning ship. When the levers went over, the two steel fish carrying their warheads streaked through the water towards the target. A breathless hush enveloped everyone as they gazed across the grey stretch of sea between the two ships. In a few seconds the torpedoes were there, burying themselves into the starboard side of the hull under the bridge. A third torpedo in the same target area must have almost cut her in two, because minutes later *Trinidad* slowly moved forward and down. From the main and after masts the large battle ensigns still flaunted their emblems as though in defiance of the enemy and the flames below them. From a signal halyard on the main mast a short line of flags fluttered in the breeze, broadcasting her last message to the world: 'I am sailing to the westward.'

On the decks of the destroyers the survivors watched in silent thought, knowing that within the sinking hull a great number of their shipmates were being committed to the deep. As the water reached the bridge the stern lifted clear and there she hung suspended for a few seconds as if reluctant to die. Then with a rush she plunged forward and down in a cloud of smoke and steam. It was twenty past one on the morning of 15 May – Ascension Day.

The best of modern equipment had gone into the construction of this ship making it a highly sophisticated fighting unit which had been tested and proved in action. Toil and enthusiasm, endurance and courage had been the sinews of her existence. Now it was gone. In minutes, only an expanding circle of turbulent water marked the grave of this memorable cruiser, a tragic memorial to a gallant ship. In seven months she had packed in more action than many of her sisters that had sailed the seas for as many years. *Trinidad* would now descend 1400 feet to lie in the calm darkness of the ocean bed. There she would become shrouded in weeds and entombed in concretions which would spread over her like a cancerous growth. This lonely war grave would become the haunt for multitudes of sea creatures, which would explore her silent cabins and mess decks for all time. Away out of gun range, the snooper planes and a few torpedo bombers had stayed to watch the end.

At the same time as the casualty list was being drawn up, Harper and Ideson were sitting on the quarter-deck drinking hot tea which *Somali*'s crew had brewed up for them. The duffel-coated stranger whom they had hauled aboard from *Trinidad* then came over and said, 'May I be allowed to sit with you chaps?' They immediately made room for him, and when he was settled he turned to them with a smile and said, 'You lads probably don't know me and I hope you won't throw me overboard when I tell you who I am. You see, I'm rather a Jonah,

Trinidad is the fifth ship that has gone under me – I'm Admiral Bonham-Carter.'

He talked for some time until a *Somali* officer came along to fetch him. By now the four destroyers, crammed with survivors, were becoming increasingly aware of the German reconnaissance planes which continuously shadowed just out of range. The speed of both *Foresight* and *Forester* was still limited by the boiler damage received in the defence of *Edinburgh*. No one could have foreseen that in four months' time *Somali* would be torpedoed in these same waters, with the loss of forty men, or that in another three months Italian aircraft in the Mediterranean would dive-bomb and destroy *Foresight*. Only *Matchless* and *Forester* would survive the war, the former to be sold into the Turkish navy and the latter broken up for scrap as soon as hostilities were over.

Soon another wave of Junkers approached and subjected the four destroyers and especially *Foresight* to further bombardment. The fact that the ship escaped a direct hit was due to the avoiding action taken by Commander Salter. An illustration of his coolness and self-control under attack was clearly shown during the brief lulls between each stick of bombs, when he calmly picked off seagulls from the bridge using a home-made catapult with dried peas as ammunition. The Admiral decided that the destroyers should seek the protection of the fleet as soon as possible. Accordingly he instructed a signal to be sent to Scapa Flow asking the commander-in-chief for assistance from his covering force. A standard broadcast of the signal was also sent to all ships in the hope that it would be picked up by one of them and retransmitted.

At the same time a discouraging incoming signal

indicated that four German cruisers with destroyer escort had set out from Norway with the intention of intercepting the British destroyers. As the hours passed, unidentified ships were reported approaching from the south, and sightings of these ships were to be expected within the hour. The crews of the destroyers loaded their guns and stood ready, watching the horizon with anxious eyes. Sure enough, within the hour eight or nine specks appeared on the horizon. The passing minutes turned the specks into ships as they came closer. The crews and survivors feared that here was yet another misfortune and one that could only have a tragic ending, but no one dared express such a thought because in every sense they were all in the same boat. Instead there was a calm acceptance of the inevitable.

Following a rapid exchange of signals between the four destroyers, *Foresight*, *Forester* and *Matchless* turned away from the approaching ships. But not *Somali*. She was the only ship left with a full quota of torpedoes and bravely she turned to the south to meet the oncoming forces. The intention was evident: if these were the German ships, *Somali* would intercept and engage them in a suicidal attempt to give a little time to the other three destroyers to escape westwards. One little destroyer, crammed with survivors, would face what appeared to be the biggest cruisers of the German fleet with only her 4.7-inch guns to do battle.

Then from the distant ships came little flashing pinpoints of light. Were these the first gun flashes of the enemy? The seconds ticked by, yet no shells fell around them. Then a great cheer went up from everyone. It could now be seen that the flashes were from signalling lamps, identifying the ships as units of the British 10th

Cruiser Squadron. It seemed almost unbelievable at first, but as the vessels neared there was no mistaking the shape of the huge cruisers. *Kent*, *Norfolk*, *Liverpool* and *Nigeria*, flying the flag of Rear-Admiral Burroughs and escorted by five destroyers, had arrived in the nick of time to shepherd the group back to Iceland. Within a very short time the forces joined to form a wide arrowhead with the four cruisers in the van in two columns.

If the Germans had earlier licked their lips over the tempting morsels presented by *Trinidad* and her four escorts, they would now be drooling at the prospect of the full meal presented by this large concentration of British ships. From the Luftwaffe's long-range air bases at Bardufoss and Banak, formations of aircraft were now taking off for their 300-mile journey to intercept. Inside an hour the air was filled with the roar of aircraft diving out of the lowering clouds. The concentration of anti-aircraft fire from the British ships was massive, yet the German pilots never faltered in their attacks. Roaring down through the intense flak in almost vertical dives they droppped their bombs then levelled off and climbed out of danger. Walls of water thrown up by the near misses at times completely hid one or another of the cruisers now bearing the brunt of the attack.

But as the hours passed and the distance from the enemy airfields increased, the attacks became less frequent; all ships survived the blitzing and came through unscathed.

CHAPTER ELEVEN

The Battered PQ16

The loss of *Edinburgh* and *Trinidad*, two vitally important cruisers, within two weeks of one another came as highly disturbing news to Admiral Tovey. After he and Admiral Bonham-Carter had fully discussed the situation it was agreed that recommendations should be made to the Admiralty that convoys be suspended until aerodromes in north Norway were neutralized or until autumn and winter darkness afforded some protection. 'But if they must continue,' he bluntly told the Admiralty, 'then very serious and heavy losses must be expected.' Admiral Sir Dudley Pound, the First Sea Lord, was fully in agreement with the conclusion and lost no time in expressing this point of view to the War Cabinet.

However, an agreement had been signed in Moscow in 1941 that a specified quantity of goods would be delivered to the USSR by 30 June 1942, most of it being supplied by the United States. The Russians insisted that the agreement be honoured. Furthermore, the heavy losses recently sustained had led to a backlog of loaded ships in Iceland waiting for escorts to Murmansk. Winston Churchill wrote to President Roosevelt presenting the serious convoy situation and the regrettable accumulation of shipping in Iceland. He trusted that the president would understand that the Admiralty was doing everything possible to meet the emergency. In reply he received an urgent cable expressing concern at the delay in supplies reaching the Sovet Union: 'We have made such a tremendous effort to get our supplies going, that to have them blocked . . . seems to me a serious mistake.' Roosevelt also expressed the opinion that 'any word reaching Stalin at this time that our supplies were stopping for any reason would have a most unfortunate effect', and that there were already 107 ships 'now loaded or being loaded in the United Kingdom and the United States prior to June lst'.

On 2 May a perturbed Mr Churchill replied explaining that the president's request to speed up the convoys was beyond the British Admiralty's power to fulfil. Destroyer escorts were already stretched to the limit, but the main problem was the ever-present threat of the enemy's heavy ships and destroyers. He pleaded with the president 'not to press us beyond our judgement in this operation which we have studied most intently and of which we have not yet been able to measure the full strain. Three convoys every two months with either thirty-five or twenty-five ships in each convoy . . . represent the extreme limit of what we can handle.'

But even this far exceeded what the First Sea Lord considered acceptable. However much Roosevelt and Churchill would have preferred Stalin to remain unaware of the true situation, the Russian leader was well informed. In a letter to Churchill of 6 May, while expressing some sympathy with the situation, he came straight to the point. Information had reached him that some ninety ships loaded with war materials for the USSR were bottled up in Iceland or in the approaches from America to Iceland, and that there was a danger that the sailing of these ships might be delayed because of the difficulty of organizing naval escorts. Stalin concluded: 'I am fully aware of the difficulties involved and of the sacrifices made by Great Britain in this matter. I feel, however, it is incumbent upon me to approach you with the request to take all possible measures in order to ensure the arrival of all the above mentioned materials in the USSR as this is extremely important for our front.'

There was no doubt as to the urgency of the request. Now that the terrible weather conditions of the Russian front were improving, the German armies were once again on the move. In reply Churchill assured Stalin that 'we are resolved to fight our way through to you with the maximum amount of war materials. We are throwing all our available resources into the solution of this problem, have dangerously weakened our Atlantic convoy escorts for this purpose, and, as you are no doubt aware, have suffered severely.'

The delicate political situation was aptly summed up by Churchill in a letter to the Chiefs of Staff Committee of 17 May:

> Not only Premier Stalin but President Roosevelt will object very much to our desisting from running the convoys now. The Russians are in heavy action, and will expect us to run the risk and pay the price entailed by our contribution. The United States ships are queueing up. My own feeling, mingled with much anxiety, is that the convoy ought to sail on the 18th. The operation is justified if a half gets through. Failure on our part to make the attempt would weaken our influence with both our major Allies. There are always the uncertainty of weather and luck, which may aid us. I share your misgivings but I feel it is a matter of duty.

As will be seen from the fate suffered by a later convoy, the number of ships that would be lost was tragically underestimated. For the officers and men of the Royal and merchant navies who were expected to 'fight their way through', the Murmansk run would live up to the name it acquired – 'Gateway to Hell'.

However much the Soviet leader grumbled about the need for larger and more frequent convoys, the following figures are a conclusive answer to those who had suggested that Britain's efforts to help Russia in her struggle were half-hearted. By mid 1942, the total American and British supplies delivered by the merchant ships of both nations, escorted by the Royal Navy, was 24,400 vehicles, 3,276 tanks, 2,665 aircraft, 615,000 tons of ammunition and miscellaneous stores, and 70,000 tons of oil and petrol – materials which could ill be spared in view of Britain's endeavours to launch a Second Front in Europe. As Churchill said, 'We gave our heart's blood resolutely to our valiant suffering Ally.'

It was therefore with serious misgivings that Admiral Tovey set about organizing the next convoy, PQ 16, to Murmansk. Consisting of thirty-five ships, it was due to sail from Iceland on 21 May under Commodore H. N. Gale, RD, RNR, in the SS *Ocean Voice*. It was in fact the largest convoy yet assembled and in line with the British prime minister's pledge to President Roosevelt. PQ16 sailed as planned with an escort of five destroyers, five corvettes, the minesweeper *Hazard* and four large trawlers, *Retriever*, *Lady Madeleine*, *Northern Wave* and *St Elstan*, all under the command of Commander Onslow in the destroyer *Ashanti*. Giving close cover west of Bear Island were the cruisers *Norfolk*, *Kent*, *Liverpool* and *Nigeria* under Rear-Admiral Burrough. To intercept the German battleship *Tirpitz* should she put to sea, the British battle fleet would cruise north-east of Iceland. But however efficient the disposition of the escort forces available, its weakness lay in the absence of fighter cover over the convoy. Commitments in the war in the Mediterranean, coupled with the shortage of aircraft-carriers, meant that none could be spared for the Arctic convoys.

The first four days proved uneventful, and on 25 May, with the convoy now in formation on a broad front of eight columns, the four cruisers and their destroyer escort joined to give added protection with their combined anti-aircraft gun-power. Also in the convoy was the 7000-ton CAM merchant ship *Empire Lawrence* with a cargo of 5000 tons of military equipment and a crew of sixty-eight. The initials CAM stood for Catapult Aircraft Merchant, a primitive contrivance created to fill the gap caused by the lack of aircraft carriers. It was in effect an ordinary cargo vessel, aboard which a catapult had been fitted which could launch a Hurricane fighter plane. Its purpose – to destroy German shadowing aircraft which would report the convoy's position and course and enable U-boats and aircraft to intercept. However, once the Hurricane had been launched and the pilot had performed his task he had to come down into the sea, praying he would be rescued before he froze to death.

At 19.00 hours that evening the Germans made a coordinated attack with twenty-five bombers and fifteen Junker 88 dive-bombers, approaching from both port and starboard sides of the convoy and diving from a height of 15,000 feet with a spine-chilling whine. The

RAF pilot aboard the *Empire Lawrence* decided that conditions were suitable for him to take off. With a roar of engines and a streak of flame from the catapult platform the pilot took off, heading for the nearest enemy aircraft, while above him the sky became filled with the black smoke of bursting shells from the barrage of gunfire put up by the escorts and convoys. It was a courageous undertaking – one lone plane pitching into battle against overwhelming odds of forty to one. Flight-Lieutenant Hay tore into the Junkers and put their attack into confusion, diving in and out of their formations, firing his guns until the barrels grew hot and blasting the enemy planes with a stream of shells. Ahead of him a torpedo bomber, unaware of his approach until a hail of bullets killed the pilot, swerved violently then hit the sea and disintegrated.

Banking steeply away from the flying debris and climbing rapidly, he saw below him a formation of five preparing for an attacking run. Roaring down from 10,000 feet with enemy planes pursuing him he tore into the group with fingers pressed tightly around the firing button. The leading plane burst into flames and in a panic of confusion the remainder broke off in an effort to escape. But by now all his ammunition was used up and he was wounded in the legs. It was time to return and try to save himself. As he flew down towards the head of the convoy fleet, preparing to bale out, two American ships, mistaking him for a Junker, opened fire. He must have wondered what sort of war he'd got himself into. As he parachuted down into the icy sea his aircraft crashed some distance ahead and sank. It was only by the prompt action of the destroyer *Volunteer* that he was rescued before he succumbed to the sub-zero temperature.

During the next three hours the Junkers intensified their attacks despite the massive barrage from the convoy. Miraculously, none of the ships was hit, and at 22.30 that day the attack faded out. The planes had however succeeded in driving the convoy into a concentration of U-boats, which torpedoed SS *Syros*. Twenty-eight out of her crew of thirty-seven were rescued by the efforts of the minesweeper *Hazard* and the rescue trawler *Lady Madeleine*.

At 02.00 on the morning of the 26th, PQ16 was 200 miles south-west of Bear Island and, following his instructions, Rear-Admiral Burrough withdrew his cruiser force and headed for the patrol area between the convoy and the Norwegian coast, taking up position to intercept any heavy German force that might have set out to attack. This substantial withdrawal meant that the anti-aircraft defence power of the escorts and convoy was sadly reduced, but with few options open to him Admiral Tovey decided he had no alternative.

Very early on the morning of the 27th, in the cold sunshine of a typical Arctic spring day when morning, noon and night have no marked difference, another attack developed, with sixty high level bombers taking part.

The first ship to go was the SS *Alamar*, followed quickly by the American *Mormacsul*. Minutes later the Russian tanker *Stari Bolshevik* was set on fire; as she trailed along at the rear of the convoy under a pillar of black smoke her crew, which included women, fought the flames with great courage, refusing to abandon her. Near misses badly damaged the American *City of Joliet* and the British

Empire Baffin, and the Polish destroyer *Garland* received a saturated bombing attack, with four bombs falling on her. The first exploded on contact and detonated the other three in the air, killing or wounding practically all the forward guns' crews in a hail of splinters.

A welcome lull for a few hours allowed the convoy's crews to snatch some sleep, but later that day another attack developed in which the ammunition ship *Empire Purcell* was hit by two bombs and blew up in a mighty holocaust of flame and black smoke. Minutes later a torpedo plunged into the hold of the *Lowther Castle* which quickly sunk.

At 13,15 that afternoon the bombers concentrated their attack on one ship, the *Empire Lawrence*, which sank after being hit by six bombs. The details of that attack given by one of the survivors, Second Officer N. S. Hulse, are worth recording:

There were about 40 planes attacking the rear of the convoy and at 13.50 I saw three planes flying in 'V' formation straight at us. They approached at about 4000 feet diving to 100 feet before releasing their bombs. I heard two bombs whistle over the bridge and explode in No 2 hatch.

As the bombs hit the ship there was a terrific explosion, all electricity failed but the steering gear was intact. The captain ordered me to lower the boats and prepare to abandon ship. We had two lifeboats . . . and as the ship lost way, the crew climbed into the port lifeboat which was lowered into the water. Someone shouted that we were again being dive bombed and we threw ourselves on to the deck as three planes dived at us dropping four bombs which hit the ship in the engine room and on the after deck. There was another terrific explosion and the magazine blew up and I felt the deck split under me. The starboard boat was blown clear of the ship which rapidly sank. It turned upside down and I saw one or two of the crew hanging on to this boat so I decided to jump and as I jumped I saw splashes from machine gun bullets hit the water. The port lifeboat had its stern and bow cut off by a bomb and many of the crew were killed in this boat. The 3rd engineer was badly wounded by machine gun bullets.

Second Officer Hulse swam, floated and scrambled around in the oil and wreckage for fifteen minutes before he managed to climb on to a raft that had broken away from the ship. During this period he saw the trawler *Lady Madeleine* picking up survivors and after another fifteen minutes the corvette *Hyderabad* found him and hauled him aboard. During this rescue the commodore's ship, *Ocean Voice*, was hit and set aflame, the bomb blowing a huge hole in her side.

Over the next three days the convoy was subjected to continuous attacks, and anxiety grew about the lowering stocks of ammunition. Early on the morning of the 28th the *City of Joliet* sank as a result of the damage she had sustained from the earlier bombing. On the afternoon of the 30th the convoy reached the entrance to the Kola inlet where another heavy air attack developed, but Russian planes appeared and broke up the German assault. Unfortunately, in the apparent safety of the inlet, the *Steel Worker* hit a mine and sank.

At six that evening the merchant navy survivors were

landed on the quay. Battered, exhausted and shivering from the cold wind, they huddled together hoping they would soon receive the warmth, hot food and sleep they so badly needed. However, there they stayed until ten o'clock the following morning when an official from the Ministry of Transport arrived and admitted that he did not know what to do with them. Eventually they were transferred to an old camp where for the next six days they barely survived on pine-needle tea and raw fat pork before being returned in small parties to Britain.

CHAPTER TWELVE

The Approaching Climax: the Carnage of PQ17

The misgivings that Admiral Tovey had expressed about PQ16 had proved well founded. Could the loss of so many precious lives, 75,000 tons of shipping and 50,000 tons of valuable cargo in one convoy be considered acceptable? His view that unless adequate air protection could be provided the convoys should be suspended until the arrival of winter darkness was not shared by the cabinet. Sacrifices in men and materials was the price that Britain had to pay. Were not the Americans in the Pacific paying a terrible price in their bitter fight against the Japanese after the débâcle of Pearl Harbor? Were not the Russians losing thousands of men on their battle-torn fronts, losses which by the end of the war would amount to twenty millions?

At the same time, however, there were growing misgivings among the naval staff as to the Germans' intentions in the coming weeks and months. Intelligence received by the Admiralty revealed that the German Naval Command were considering mounting a combined offensive during the summer months using aircraft and U-boats westward of Bear Island and heavy surface ships to the east. This was something the Admiralty had always feared. Until now the Royal Navy's heavy ships had limited their protective screen to the west of Bear Island rather than subject them to concentrated U-boat attacks from North Cape bases. This also placed them in a strategic position to counter any attack launched by the *Tirpitz* and her consorts. But if the enemy now implemented their planned offensive then the next convoy to Russia would be in grave danger.

Intelligence information was gathered from two main sources: transmissions from secret agents parachuted or coast-landed into enemy-occupied territory; and the successful decoding of German secret signals by means of 'Enigma'.

Secret agents in the occupied territories worked under the aegis of the Special Operations Executive (SOE), London. Of those working in Holland as many as half were caught and either executed or imprisoned by the German security forces, while in France only one per cent were ever discovered. In Norway SOE operations were able to provide vital information on the planned activities of the German Naval Command and the Norwegian-based Luftwaffe. The information, transmitted to the Admiralty by these daring and courageous men and women, was the means of saving the lives of hundreds of Royal Navy and merchant seamen.

Much has been written about British agents working in Germany, France and Norway, but the Germans themselves were not slow in establishing similar cells to gain information, though agents planted in Britain were not generally successful. Almost every German agent from 1941 to 1945 was constantly under the vigilant eyes of the British Secret Intelligence Service, MI5. A typical example of this is given by Captain Jack Broome in his book *Convoy is to Scatter*. His destroyer, *Keppel*, received a signal from the Admiralty with the information that a German secret agent, observed in Greenock, was thought to have stolen a boat and to be making for the Irish Free State with important information regarding the sailing of the next Russian convoy. Captain Broome's orders were to find it before the man landed. With less than an hour to go before dusk the chance of finding a small boat in the hundreds of square miles of the Irish Sea were infinitesimal, but he nevertheless raced due south on a line between the Mull and Larne. Just before dark and only a mile or two from the Irish coast, *Keppel* came upon the boat. The occupant exactly fitted the description of the agent, and after being taken aboard and interrogated he admitted who he was.

The other main source of enemy intelligence was the 'Enigma' machine, a German encoder/decoder which was prototyped as early as 1926 and modified in 1937. Its importance lay in the fact that any messages encoded on it could not be deciphered without the use of the same machine. Before the war began, in a coordinated secret research operation between the French and Polish services, a duplicate machine was constructed, so that when the war broke out the British Intelligence Service already had it in their possession. By this means they were able to intercept, decode and have advance information of German plans and objectives.

The information received by the Admiralty in June 1942 led Churchill to make tentative proposals to the First Sea Lord that to counter the expected German offensive it would be advisable to bring in the aircraft-carriers *Indomitable*, *Victorious*, *Argus* and *Eagle* from Malta and to add to them auxiliary carriers and twenty-five destroyers as well as two 16-inch battleships. The next convoy would then fight its way through to Murmansk under a massive air umbrella.

This proposed showdown with the enemy might have been successful, but the cost in carriers and battleships would have proved prohibitive. Also, to have brought these forces to the Arctic would have critically weakened the whole Mediterranean strategy. While in the modern idiom 'it seemed a good idea at the time', Churchill failed to convince his colleagues and later wrote: 'I could not however persuade my Admiralty friends to take this kind of line, which of course involved engaging a force vital to us out of proportion to the actual military importance of the Arctic convoys.' The impracticability of this proposed perilous and venturesome undertaking was later summed up by Admiral Tovey:

> The strategical situation thus produced was wholly favourable to the enemy. His heavy ships would be operating close to their own coast, with the support of powerful shore based air reconnaissance and striking forces, and protected, if so desired, by a screen of U-boats in the channels between Spitzbergen and Norway. Our covering forces on the other hand, if they entered these waters, would be without shore-based air support, one thousand miles from their base and with their destroyers too short of fuel to escort a damaged ship to harbour.

Lengthy discussions took place between government and Admiralty on the course of action to be adopted when the next convoy, PQ17, sailed. A variety of solutions to defeat the Germans' plan were proposed by Admiral Tovey but all were discounted. Admiral Tovey then learned that the First Sea Lord was seriously considering a manoeuvre whereby PQ17, if attacked by a German naval force that included the great battleship *Tirpitz*, would be given the order to scatter. The plan came as a bombshell to Admiral Tovey, for it was an accepted principle in ocean warfare that when a convoy is confronted by a force far outweighing the power of its escorts to deal with then such a plan is only feasible if a large ocean area is available in which to operate. The circumstances in the Barents Sea were far different, since the ice barrier to the north and the German bases to the south prevented ships escaping from the concentrated attentions of U-boats, dive-bombers and torpedo-carrying aircraft based in Norway.

Instructions given to Admiral Tovey were clear. Surface forces would defend the convoy to the west of Bear Island but if a surface attack by *Tirpitz* and her consorts developed east of that point then the defence would have to depend on Allied submarines. But the question remained – how could the fast-moving *Tirpitz* with her massive armour-plating be stopped or even slowed in her bid to annihilate the merchant ships and their comparatively feeble escorts?

In the meantime, German Naval Command had completed their plan to attack the next convoy to Murmansk in force. Their fleet would be divided into two groups: the Trondheim group made up of the battleship *Tirpitz*, the cruiser *Hipper* and six destroyers; and the Narvik group comprising the pocket battleships *Lutzow* (formerly *Deutschland*) and *Scheer* and six destroyers. In addition a fleet of U-boats would operate in the Barents Sea to intercept and report. The strength of the Luftwaffe in north Norway at this time was 260 aircraft comprising

Junker and Stuka dive-bombers, Heinkel torpedo bombers and Condor long-range reconnaissance aircraft.

The plan was simple enough. The Trondheim group would proceed northward along the coast to Vestfiord near Narvik and the Narvik group would move northward to Altenfiord. On receipt of a coded signal both groups would sail to rendezvous in the Barents Sea some miles north of North Cape and from there attack the convoy which by that time would be east of Bear Island. The *Tirpitz* and *Hipper* would concentrate on the escort forces while the *Lutzow* and *Scheer* would sink as many merchant ships as possible. Any that were crippled or managed to escape could be dealt with by the U-boats and the Luftwaffe. The plan had every hope of success, for east of Bear Island escape was virtually impossible because of the ice barrier to the north. The strait through which the convoy had to sail was only 300 miles wide and well within striking distance of the Norwegian airfields.

The two convoys sailed as planned on 27 June, the eastward-bound PQ17 under Commodore J. Dowding, RNR, and the returning convoy QP13, of thirty-five ships, under Commodore N. Gale, RNR. On the afternoon of 2 July the two convoys passed one another west of Bear Island, with PQ17 heading north of it. Units of the home fleet, comprised of the battleship *Duke of York*, flying the flag of Admiral Tovey, the United States battleship *Washington*, the carrier *Victorious*, two cruisers and fourteen destroyers, held a position to the north of the convoy routes. A little to the south was a cruiser force under the command of Rear-Admiral Hamilton, comprised of the *London*, the *Norfolk*, the two US cruisers, *Wichita* and *Tuscaloosa*, two US destroyers, *Wainwright*

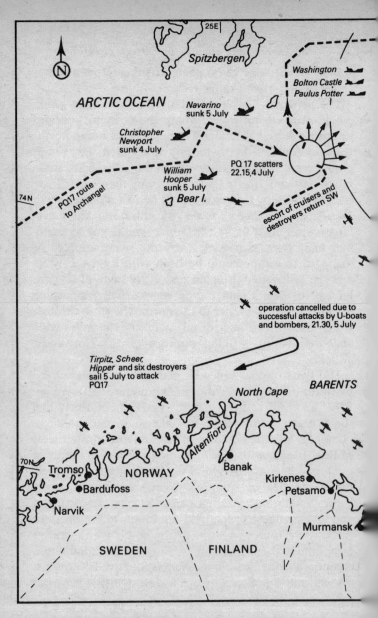

The Massacre of Convoy PQ17
4 to 10 July 1942

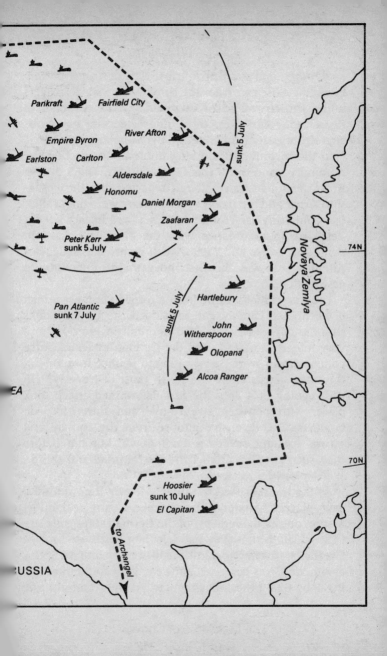

Pankraft

Fairfield City

Empire Byron

River Afton

Earlston   Carlton

Aldersdale

Honomu

Daniel Morgan

Zaafaran

Peter Kerr
sunk 5 July

Pan Atlantic
sunk 7 July

Hartlebury

John
Witherspoon

Olopana

Alcoa Ranger

sunk 5 July

sunk 5 July

Novaya Zemlya

74N

EA

70N

Hoosier
sunk 10 July

El Capitan

to Archangel

RUSSIA

and *Rowan*, and the British tribal class destroyer *Somali*. Providing close escort for the convoy were six destroyers under the command of Commander Jack Broome in *Keppel*, four corvettes, three minesweepers, two anti-aircraft ships, four trawlers and two submarines.

In the meantime disturbing information reached the Admiralty concerning the German ships. On 3 July a British reconnaissance aircraft reported that the battleship *Tirpitz* and the heavy cruiser *Hipper* were not at their usual moorings at Trondheim. They had in fact left for Vestfiord, in accordance with the planned operation, while the *Scheer* and *Lutzow* with escort had sailed for Altenfiord. It was the first move in the operation to destroy PQ17.

The first casualty came from a torpedo bomber which dived on the convoy and torpedoed the United States ship *Christopher Newport*. The Admiralty were now in a very uneasy situation. Had the German attacking force gone to sea or were they waiting to pounce from one of the many fiords along the north coast of Norway? On the evening of 4 July the first determined attack took place, with between twenty-five and thirty torpedo bombers. The defensive gunfire from the convoy and escorts brought several aircraft down, but not before they succeeded in sinking the SS *Navarino* and the SS *William Hooper*.

As the hours passed the unease felt by the Admiralty gave place to anxiety. The absence of any real information on the movements of the German ships gave rise to speculation that they had left their berths and might already be heading towards the ill-starred convoy. If this assumption was correct then the enemy could intercept PQ17 by 02.00 the following day. At the Admiralty the

First Sea Lord in conference with chiefs of staff considered the options open to them. There were only three:

1. – To reverse the convoy's course and to send in the main battle fleet with the aircraft carrier *Victorious*. To do this would mean that the heavy ships would face confrontation with the whole weight of the Northern German Air Force and place them in the centre of U-boat concentrations. The aircraft that could be launched from *Victorious* were far inferior to the Luftwaffe planes, which could be flown off from their nearby bases in Norway. To place the capital ships and a carrier in this impossible situation would lead to a useless sacrifice and one which the Admiralty were determined to avoid.

2. – To withdraw the cruisers, which alone could not possibly hope to match the *Tirpitz*, and allow the convoy with its destroyer escort to proceed on its course. If the German ships did come upon them their only hope of partial survival would lie in a heavy screen provided by Captain Broome's destroyers and their torpedo attacks. In any event it would be a massacre, with only the hope of a few ships escaping the massive fire-power of the *Tirpitz* with her eight 15-inch, twelve 5.9-inch, sixteen 4-inch and seventy-four smaller guns.

3. – To order the convoy to scatter in the hope that the German ships would find it more difficult to track individual ships and at the same time be unwilling to roam around the Barents Sea too long in case a British force should cut off their retreat. Again, heavy casualties would be inevitable, and

once the merchant ships had dispersed it would be impossible to collect them again to form a united defence against air and U-boat attack. As separate units they would be sitting ducks.

Never before had the conference had to debate such a harrowing issue, and it was some time before a final decision was reached. In the mind of the First Sea Lord there was only one solution, the dispersal of the convoy. His opinion was not shared by the main body of the conference, but despite their arguments he gave the order for the cruisers to withdraw to the west and for the convoy to disperse. It was an order which in the long history of the Admiralty was considered to be one of the most disastrous ever made.

The order was received by Captain Broome in *Keppel*, commanding the close destroyer escort, Admiral Hamilton in *London*, commanding the cruiser squadron, and the commander-in-chief Admiral Tovey in *Duke of York*, commanding the battle fleet. The signal read as follows: 'Immediate. Owing to threat from surface ships, convoy is to disperse and proceed to Russian ports.' When Captain Broome received it he was bewildered. It was so inconclusive. Was the threatened attack imminent? What were his own orders? And the term 'Russian ports' was also confusing – there was only one, Archangel, for Murmansk had been reduced to a smoking ruin by enemy air attacks.

Thirteen minues later bewilderment turned to shock when another signal arrived: 'Secret. Most immediate. Convoy is to scatter.' The full implications of the order suddenly came home to him. It could only mean that in the intervening thirteen minutes the situation had rapidly deteriorated, that the Admiralty had received further information confirming immediate overwhelming attack, and that the defenceless merchant ships would stand a better chance individually against enemy U-boats and aircraft.

Admiral Hamilton was only five miles from the convoy and Admiral Tovey some 350 miles away when they received the signal. Both were convinced from the wording that attack was imminent, and bridge lookouts on *Keppel* and *London* were already scanning the horizon for the first sign of the enemy ships. The task of passing the message to the commodore of the merchant navy fleet was deeply distressing to Captain Broome. But the order had to be obeyed, and he made the fateful signal to the SS *River Afton*: 'Convoy is to scatter.'

To Commodore John Dowding the instruction was almost unbelievable. Twice he asked for the order to be repeated. When it was confirmed he assumed that the enemy must be almost upon them, and without hesitation he signalled the convoy to scatter. This they did in a brilliantly executed movement, fanning out to every point of the compass from north to east and from east to south-east. Captain Broome with his consorts still had no clear indication as to what he was expected to do. Stay to defend the convoy? What convoy? The merchant ships were now spreading out at top speed into the Barents Sea and would soon be scattered over hundreds of square miles of ocean. A subsequent signal indicated that the smaller escorts were to proceed independently to Archangel. But what of the destroyers? In the absence of any direct orders, Captain Broome signalled Admiral Hamilton that he proposed to join him. The signal in fact sought clarification and guidance on his next move. On receiving the reply 'Approved', *Keppel* with her five consorts increased speed to join the cruiser squadron that could be seen heading south-west. If a battle with the German fleet was imminent then Admiral Hamilton would need all the destroyer support possible. Little did they know that the Admiralty instructions were based on conjecture rather than on definite information. At the time the fateful signal was received by *Keppel*, at 21.36 on 4 July, the German ships were in fact still anchored at Altenfiord and it was not until noon on the 5th that Hitler gave permission for the fleet to put to sea.

The Germans were not long in taking full advantage of the situation. Dive-bombers and torpedo bombers setting out from Norway were now in no danger from the concentrated fire of a well-guarded convoy, and U-boats could surface and freely attack the plodding merchant ships. On the morning of 5 July the massacre began, and during the next five days and nights of perpetual daylight the little ships were subjected to the most vicious attacks of the Arctic War. High level bombers, dive-bombers and U-boats hounded the defenceless vessels and few escaped. It would take another book to recount the stories of courage, heroism and tragedy that took place in this most melancholy episode of the naval war. Of the thirty-five ships that left Iceland, twenty-four were sunk with many of their crew perishing in the icy sea or suffering mutilation from frostbite. Only two British, six American, one Panamanian and two Russian merchant ships survived to reach Archangel. Of the shipping losses, fourteen were American.

The wolf-pack of U-boats that had been shadowing the convoy and had, much to their delight and amazement, watched the convoy's escorts disappear over the horizon, now set about the annihilation of PQ17. Contemptuously ignoring the feeble resistance put up by the merchant navy's gunners with their 4-inch guns, they moved in. Among the early victims were the *Bolton Castle, Earlston, Empire Byron, Washington* and the commodore's ship *River Afton*. Then the Luftwaffe also decided to join the hunt. In a coordinated attack with the U-boats they launched over 200 Junker 88 dive bombers and Heinkel torpedo bombers. It was literally a turkey shoot. During that afternoon and early evening they sank the *Peter Kerr, Pankraft, Fairfield City, Aldersdale, Daniel Morgan, Zaafaran* and *Honomu,* leaving the *Paulus Potter* badly damaged but still afloat only to be sunk a few days later as she neared the Russian coast.

By the morning of 6 July fourteen merchant vessels had been sunk without loss to the enemy. However much the remnants of the convoy might try to shake off pursuit, it was now obvious that they would eventually have to set a course for the Novaya Zemlya coast, and all the Germans had to do was to race ahead and intercept them. In the next three or four days aircraft and submarines sank the *Hartlebury, Pan Atlantic, John Witherspoon, Alcoa Ranger, Carlton, Olopana, Hoosier* and the *El Capitan.* The eleven surviving ships, *Ocean Freedom, Samuel Chase, Benjamin Harrison, Donbass, Bellingham, Winston Salem, Empire Tide, Silver Sword, Troubadour, Azerbaijan* and *Ironclad* set out speedily for the nearest land, Novaya Zemlya, 500 miles south-east, hoping to escape the attentions of the enemy. For the survivors of the twenty-four sunken ships it was a cruel and distressing voyage across an ocean now dotted with many boats each containing sick and wounded men, most plucked from the icy seas and barely surviving in the bitter wind. It was a miracle of survival and endurance that from an approximate crew total of 1500 men, 1300 reached Novaya Zemlya.

The story cannot close without reference to the remarkable courage and initiative of Commodore John Dowding. After his ship the SS *River Afton* had been sunk, the little corvette *Lotus* turned back to look for survivors and found the commodore sitting on a raft in icy water with two members of the crew. Reaching the Matochkin Strait which separates the two halves of Novaya Zemlya, *Lotus* found one or two other ships which had survived. Deciding that the anchorage was unsafe, *Lotus* and her charges set sail again and after further bombing attacks, eventually reached Archangel.

Hardly had they reached the safety of the port than Commodore Dowding, convinced that survivors of his scattered convoy in open boats would by then have reached Novaya Zemlya, decided that a rescue attempt had to be made. On 16 July, he left Archangel in the corvette *Poppy*, with *Lotus* and the French *La Malouine*, and set out for the barren 400-mile-long island nearly 600 miles away. Three days later they reached the western coast and began their search. Probing into every inlet, their efforts were well rewarded. Five or six men in this creek, some miles further north a group in that cove, a battered ship partly beached in another, to the south among the rocks a smashed lifeboat turned upside down to form a hut sheltering another group from the icy wind – and so it went on until Commodore Dowding found the remaining ships of his convoy and over 200 survivors. After a hazardous journey southwards under constant bombing attacks the little fleet finally reached Archangel on 24 July.

The destruction of convoy PQ17 was one of the most

tragic and inexplicable events in British naval history. When the news leaked out, the repercussions in both Britain and America were grave. Charges of clumsy and ill-judged decisions against the Admiralty and the Royal Navy were made and never disposed of. None the less, the fact that the German fleet did sail with the object of intercepting and destroying the convoy should not be forgotten. At midday on 5 July the *Tirpitz*, *Scheer* and *Hipper*, with a strong escort of destroyers, had set out from Altenfiord heading north-west in the direction of Bear Island to intercept the convoy. They were soon sighted, first by a Russian submarine, which incorrectly claimed two hits on the *Tirpitz*, and later by a British submarine. Evasive action had to be taken by the German ships, and German High Command, on the incorrect assumption that they might be sailing into a trap and suffer the same fate as *Bismark* a year earlier, decided on withdrawal. From signals transmitted by their air reconnaissance and U-boats they already knew that the convoy had scattered and that British cruisers and destroyers had withdrawn. They therefore took the view, with some justification, that PQ17 could be just as effectively dealt with by a concentration of air and U-boat attacks. On the evening of the 5th, after only ten hours at sea, the fleet was ordered to return to Altenfiord.

What the result would have been if the convoy had not scattered, and the destroyers had remained to try to deal with the overwhelming might of the *Tirpitz* and her consorts, would perhaps have been equally disastrous. In retrospect it is simple enough to assess the overall situation and to know what should have been done, but at the time it was a question of each side trying to guess the other's move. A decision had to be taken, and the responsibility rested on the shoulders of the First Sea Lord. There is little doubt that history will continue to debate Admiral Sir Dudley Pound's decision, but it is less certain that it will ever reach a satisfactory conclusion.

CHAPTER THIRTEEN

The Minefield

The history of these tragic events cannot be closed without describing the story of the ill-starred homeward-bound convoy of QP13 in the last stages of its voyage. It will be remembered that QP13 passed the outward-bound PQ17 on the afternoon of 2 July as it steered a course for the northern coast of Iceland. This convoy of thirty-five merchant ships had an escort of five destroyers, *Inglefield*, *Achates*, *Volunteer*, *Intrepid* and *Garland*; four corvettes, *Stalwart*, *Honeysuckle*, *Hyderabad* and *Roseleys*; two minesweepers, *Niger* and *Hussar*, and the two trawlers *Lady Madeleine* and *St Elstan*. A group of about 400 officers and ratings survivors were distributed according to availability of accommodation among the escort vessels, about thirty in each of the destroyers and corvettes, about forty in each of the minesweepers, and sixteen in each of the trawlers.

The convoy had a quiet passage to Iceland mainly because the Germans concentrated the whole of their attack on PQ17. On 4 July, the day PQ17 received the fateful signal to scatter, QP13 arrived off the north-eastern corner of Iceland. Sixteen of the thirty-five ships were bound for Britain and turned due south along the eastern coast of the island. The remaining nineteen, led by Captain John Hiss, master of the American freighter *Robin*, who was acting as merchant fleet commodore,

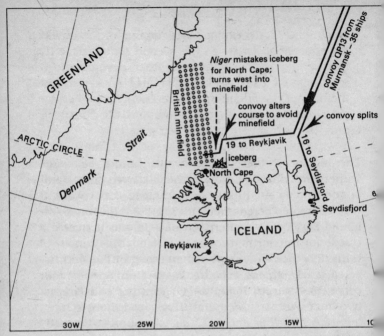

HMS *Niger* with Convoy strays into a British Minefield, 4 July 1942

were mostly American and were bound for Reykjavik on the south-west coast. As this second group made their way along the northern coast that evening the bad weather and poor visibility that had so far protected them from the attentions of the enemy now became a perilous handicap. In such conditions the convoy had only an approximate idea of their position.

At seven o'clock that evening, *Niger*, commanded by the senior officer of the escort, Group Commander Antony Cubison, RN, proceeded ahead to establish a navigational fix. He had been notified that there was a British minefield just off the north-west corner of Iceland, placed there to entrap any German vessel that attempted to break through the Denmark Straits and out into the Atlantic. Its positioning left a narrow channel ten miles wide between the southern edge of the minefield and the coastline through which ships had to pass. Cubison then signalled the acting commodore to re-form the convoy into two columns to negotiate the narrow passage. From soundings taken at the time he believed that Iceland's North Cape had been passed, so he ordered a south-west course to strike a sighting of the coast. Carefully steering through the mist and low cloud he suddenly saw something that had all the appearance of a steep cliff looming up which he assumed must be the North Cape after all. He reasoned that he must have altered the convoy's course too soon and that to continue would bring them on to the rocky coast. To rectify this he immediately signalled Captain Hiss to swing the convoy back on to a westerly course. However, barely had the merchant ships adopted the new course than a sudden clearance in the poor visibility showed that what he had assumed to be a cliff face was in fact a massive iceberg. Recognizing his mistake, Cubison was at once aware that at this point they could be in the minefield and hastily signalled the convoy to change course to the south-west.

But it was too late. Within minutes *Niger* struck a mine and blew up, her hull torn apart and her back broken. She sank very quickly, taking Commander Cubison, eighty officers and crew and thirty-nine *Edinburgh* passengers down with her. Moments later the SS *Hybert* hit a mine. Cut in two, she disappeared in a cauldron of fire. Utter confusion broke out among the ships following as one vessel after another was shaken by mighty explosions which triggered off other mines in the vicinity, creating columns of water that looked like shell splashes. The captains of the merchant ships, who were unaware of the existence of the minefields, immediately assumed they were being shelled by some distant and unseen German warship. Within minutes another vessel, the SS *Heffron*, blew up, followed by the SS *Marramer*, leaving their crews struggling in the icy water. The next victim was the SS *John Randolph*. Her bows were blown off but the inner bulkheads held the rush of water.

Now it was every ship for itelf, fighting for survival. In a wilderness of confusion, the heavy freighters, slow to answer the helm, sluggishly twisted and turned in a desperate bid to avoid catastrophe. Course alteration signals no longer existed as vessels yawed this way and that amid a wail of sirens. Then, less than half a mile away, a brilliant flash lit up the cheerless grey of the Arctic night. It was the Russian freighter *Rodina*. A mine had slammed against the starboard side, smashing through the hull and allowing tons of water to surge through the bulkheads fractured by the eruption. Slowly she listed to starboard, her decks tilting to face the other ships. As her rails dipped under, her decks were covered with people sliding and slipping, struggling to reach the lifeboats, among them many women and children. Two lifeboats drifted free, empty except for some twenty or thirty in the water with fingers locked over the gunwales.

Barely had the echoes of the *Rodina* explosion faded than the vessel astern, the SS *Exterminator*, ran on to a mine. There was no smoke or fire, just a dull boom that tore out the middle and broke her in two. The end was swift. For a few moments her bow and stern hung suspended over the water, spilling their cargo of human flotsam and thick black oil, and then with a roar of exploding boilers she disappeared, leaving only a vast cauldron of white bubbling water in the middle of a pool of oil and screaming men. The dead and the living in the water numbered over four hundred.

The two rescue trawlers *St Elstan* and *Lady Madeleine* were also in the middle of the holocaust and, like the others, totally unaware of the minefield. They came to the conclusion that a number of U-boats had intercepted them and were firing torpedoes into the group of ships. The remaining freighters were wallowing around like blinded men on a battlefield. A decision had to be made quickly in order to protect them, but when it was implemented it was itself a sentence of death for those in the sea. The two trawlers sped into the centre of the area firing a volley of depth charges. But in that span of sea where the ships had foundered there were people, terror-stricken and screaming for help, trying to swim through oil fuel. Then, in a succession of deafening booms, the depth charges exploded, hurling columns of water high into the air. The effect on those in the water was horrifying. The lucky ones died instantly, but the others . . .

St Elstan, assuming that the depth charges would deter the enemy submarines and keep them submerged, began their search for survivors, still unaware that they were moving around in the middle of a minefield. Miraculously, some of the men in the water had managed to survive the depth-charging and the cold. On top of that there was the oil, which is a vicious irritant that scorches the eyes, burns the lungs and causes violent retching which ruptures the stomach. As the *St Elstan* moved around trying to pick up those still alive, the crew hung over the side, their hands reaching out. Some survivors were able to hang on to the netting hung over the side but they were so soaked in oil and on the point of collapse that they could do nothing to help themselves and had to be line-hauled aboard.

Soon some of the other escorts arrived and joined the rescue. Among them was the *Lady Madeleine* and the Free French corvette *Roselys*, commanded by Lieutenant Bergeret. Together they circled around in the middle of the minefield for six and a half hours, rescuing 230 people of whom forty-seven later died of exposure. It was a sorrowful conclusion to one of the most lamentable episodes in naval history.

The Germans, as might be expected, had been jubilant at the success of their operation against PQ17, which they believed was due to the magnificent cooperation between the Luftwaffe and the U-boat command – credit that was hardly merited in view of the fact that there was no opposition at all, the British ships being utterly defenceless. But for the Allies the consequences of the two disastrous voyages, of PQ17 and QP13, were deeply felt not only in Britain and the United States but especially in Moscow, where the news of the loss of 130,000 tons of valuable cargo, including 400 tanks, 200 aircraft and 3300 vehicles was received with dismay and anger. America alone had lost nineteen cargo ships with a gross tonnage of approximately 115,000 tons. The Admiralty's reaction to the news was predictable: the convoys must be suspended until the period of perpetual daylight was over. The prime minister's response, however, was equally predictable: he felt it would be a grave mistake to do this, and was inclined instead 'not to lower but on the contrary to raise the stakes on the principle of "in defeat defiance"'. But he did concede that it would be wise to delay the sailing of PQ18 for a while. In the circumstances Churchill felt it necessary to inform Stalin of the disagreeable news and the singular conditions that had brought about the misfortune. In a long letter written in the most conciliatory terms he explained that:

> We do not think it right to risk our Home Fleet east of Bear Island or where it can be brought under the attack of the powerful German shore-based aircraft. If one or two of our very few most powerful battleships were to be lost or even seriously damaged while *Tirpitz* and her consorts, soon to be joined by the *Scharnhorst*, remained in action, the whole command of the Atlantic would be temporarily lost. Besides affecting the food supplies by which we live, our war effort would be crippled, and above all, the great convoys of American troops across the ocean,

rising presently to as many as 80,000 in a month, would be prevented and the building up of a really strong Second Front in 1943 rendered impossible.

Stalin was not impressed. In his reply he stated that his naval experts considered that the British justification for the cessation of convoys to the USSR was 'wholly unconvincing'. He went on:

I never expected that the British Government would stop the dispatch of war materials to us just at the very moment when the Soviet Union in view of the serious situation on the Soviet–German front requires these materials more than ever.

There was much justice in the Russian viewpoint. The Germans had mounted a massive offensive on a 200-mile front and were making advances despite the sacrificial efforts of the Russian generals to halt them. On 12 August 1942 Churchill visited Moscow where for the next five days frank and constructive talks were held with Premier Stalin. The discussions were much more friendly than the British prime minister had anticipated, with the result that on his return to London he said, 'On the whole I am definitely encouraged by my visit to Moscow.' He was impressed by Stalin's confidence in the Russians' ability to win the war, and he returned with a better understanding of the war materials Stalin needed. As a consequence, preparations were put in hand for the sailing of PQ18, which would take place early in September.

An interesting little story emerges from Churchill's memoirs of the visit, one which he tells against himself. The aircraft that carried him and Averell Harriman had to fly across the mountains of Kurdistan. As they arrived on the Teheran airfield Churchill noticed that the altimeter registered 4500 feet. 'I ignorantly remarked to the pilot — "You had better get that adjusted before we take off again", to which came the reply — "The Teheran airfield is four thousand five hundred feet above sea-level, sir".'

In the previous May a proposal had been made by the commander-in-chief of Coastal Command, Air Marshal Sir Philip Joubert, to establish a base at Murmansk comprising reconnaissance, fighter and torpedo bomber aircraft. At that time the suggestion had been discarded, but following the PQ17 fiasco it was pointed out that had these aircraft been stationed in north Russia the extent of the disaster might have been greatly reduced. As a result, thirty-two aircraft set out from Britain for north Russia in early September, a trip of 1500 miles across sea and enemy-held territory. Of these only twenty-three arrived: six crashed in Norway and Sweden, two made forced landings in Russia and one was shot down by a Russian fighter while flying over a sensitive zone. Unfortunately, one of those shot down in Scandinavia carried secret documents revealing the radio communication system to be used by the convoys of PQ18 and QP14. From this the Germans were able to build up a fairly accurate picture of the route and the schedule to be employed.

A few days earlier, the German naval commander-in-chief had held a conference with Hitler. Admiral Raeder stated that 'We can assume that our submarines and aircraft which totally destroyed the last convoy have forced the enemy to give up this route temporarily.' He further pointed out that 'supplies to northern ports of

Russia remain decisive for the whole conduct of the war waged by the Anglo-Saxons,' and he went on, 'The enemy will most probably continue to ship supplies to Northern Russia and the Naval Staff must therefore maintain submarines along the same routes. The greater part of the Fleet will also be stationed in Northern Norway.' Hitler decided that rather than venture his heavy surface ships in confrontations wih the British fleet by attacking the outward-bound convoys, it would be better to employ them on homeward-bound convoys which would be comparatively less well-guarded and therefore less of a risk – a curious decision in view of the importance he attached to eliminating the supply-line to the Soviet Union.

CHAPTER FOURTEEN

The Turning Point

Convoy PQ18, comprising forty merchant ships and heavily escorted, set sail on 2 September 1942. Altogether fifty warships were employed in its protection. They included twenty-five destroyers, nine submarines, four corvettes, two tankers, two anti-aircraft ships, four trawlers, three minesweepers, the escort carrier *Avenger* and the cruiser *Scylla*, under Rear-Admiral Burnett.

First evidence of the enemy's intentions came on the 12th, about 100 miles north-west of Bear Island, when a series of determined attacks were made by a pack of U-boats. In one of these the destroyer *Faulkner* sank U88. On the following day the two merchant ships *Stalingrad* and *Oliver Elsworth* were torpedoed and sunk. At mid afternoon came a mass attack from over ninety bombers and torpedo bombers. In fact this was one of the most concentrated torpedo-bomber attacks of the war, for at one time no less than 110 torpedoes raced towards the convoy simultaneously. Despite efforts to execute emergency turns to bring the ships parallel to the advancing torpedoes, eight were hit, one erupting in a massive explosion. In two further attacks that evening the bombers failed to score any hits, and due to the intense barrage of gunfire put up by both the escorts and merchant ships, assisted by *Scylla*'s powerful anti-aircraft guns, the Germans lost eight aircraft.

Early on the following day the tanker *Atheltemplar* was hit and had to be sunk, but this was compensated for later that day by the sinking of U589 by the destroyers *Onslow* and *Faulkner*. Late on the 14th the air battle was resumed when twenty torpedo bombers attacked, concentrating on *Scylla* and the carrier *Avenger* – clear evidence of the threat the carrier's fighters posed to the attacking bombers. In this attack the Germans lost eleven aircraft without scoring a single hit on the convoy. Almost immediately another thirty-seven torpedo bombers came over, nine of which were destroyed. Unfortunately the merchant ship *Mary Luchenback*, carrying 2000 tons of TNT, was hit and blew up with an enormous explosion that gave no chance of survival to the fifty-odd crew. In the next twenty-four hours over seventy aircraft attacked the convoy without success and in doing so lost three more planes. The convoy was now at the extreme limit of the range of the Luftwaffe's offensive capability and gradually the attacks diminished. But hardly had the exhausted gun crews relaxed than another emergency arose with the discovery that as many as twelve U-boats were around the convoy waiting for an opportunity to attack. However, such was the intensity and skill of the destroyers and corvettes in their action against the new threat that the enemy was obliged to withdraw, though not before U457 was sunk by the destroyer *Impulsive*.

With PQ18 virtually within striking distance of Murmansk, Burnett launched his plan to transfer some of his escort forces from PQ18 to the returning QP14. QP14 was a small convoy of only fifteen empty ships, headed by the *Ocean Voice* in which the courageous Commodore John Dowding hoisted his pennant. Closely escorting the convoy were two anti-aircraft ships, two destroyers, four corvettes, three minesweepers and three trawlers under the direct command of Captain J. Crombie, RN.

It will be remembered that Hitler had intended to employ his surface ships to attack returning convoys only, and to that end had assembled the battleship *Scheer*, the cruisers *Hipper* and *Köln* and a destroyer escort at Altenfiord ready to move out when called upon. Captain Crombie's escort group of little ships was not exactly a formidable force which the German fleet might hesitate to engage, yet when the opportunity to strike arose Hitler warned Admiral Raeder against risking the fleet without gaining commensurate successes. Raeder was well aware of the existence of a British submarine force off north Norway as well as the battleships at sea and the new force of torpedo bombers based in Russia, and he was not prepared to take the risk of incurring Hitler's wrath if things should go wrong. He therefore cancelled the intended foray into the Barents Sea.

In the meantine QP14 moved steadily westward, and on the 18th Burnett joined the convoy with the carrier *Avenger* and the cruiser *Scylla* and a flotilla of destroyers. By this time the convoy was well beyond the range of enemy aircraft, and he decided to return *Avenger* and his flagship *Scylla* to base and transfer his flag to the destroyer *Milne*, commanded by Captain I. M. R. Campbell, RN. Within an hour or so of the two ships' departure, a trailing U-boat succeeded in torpedoing the tribal class destroyer *Somali*, commanded by Lieutenant-Commander C. D. Maud, RN. The weather was good and as the destroyer still remained afloat there seemed an excellent chance of saving her. In the event she was taken in tow by her sister ship *Ashanti*, commanded by Captain R. Onslow, RN, and proceeded under the escort of three destroyers and a trawler.

On the 22nd, with everything seemingly going well, Burnett in *Milne* set course for Scapa Flow. Hardly had he departed than another U-boat infiltrated the screen and torpedoed three ships, the tanker *Gray Ranger*, the freighter *Bellingham* and the commodore's vessel *Ocean Voice*. Once again John Dowding found himself swimming around in the ice-cold sea. Within a short time the attendant rescue ships were at hand and most of the officers and crew of the sunken vessels were picked up.

Meanwhile the torpedoed *Somali*, under tow, was making steady progress westward albeit at only 5 knots. Hundreds of tons of water had poured through the torpedo hole into the engine and boiler rooms, setting her deep in the water and affecting her buoyancy. Despite this, there still seemed a fair chance of making port. Then on the 23rd the weather changed. As evening drifted into Arctic night the wind rose higher, whistling and whining in the rigging. The wave troughs steepened and deepened, with long braids of white streaking across the green surface, their tops whisked into spume by the wind. Soon the ship was nothing more than a waterlogged hulk settling deeper under the impact of each wave.

The two captains watched anxiously as the tow whipped out of the water, hurling a shower of spray as it pulled momentarily taut and then plunged back into the sea. Each time it lifted to bar-tautness, trembling under the strain, it seemed on the point of breaking. As the oncoming rollers lifted the bows to run swiftly under the ship, a screeching noise of creaking and jarring metal came from the tortured bulkheads amidships. It was obvious that it was only a matter of time before disaster struck. As a precautionary measure, Lieutenant-Commander Maud ordered all hands on deck. All but eighty had already been taken off some hours earlier. Minutes later, in an agonizing scream of ruptured metal, the ship broke in half, the two parts drifting away and sinking, and in spite of a swift rescue attempt, only thirty-five men, including Lieutenant-Commander Maud, were picked up.

During the whole operation against PQ18 and QP14 the Germans lost forty-one aircraft and four U-boats. A further five U-boats were damaged. On the British side sixteen merchant ships, a destroyer, a minesweeper and a tanker had been lost. It was a costly battle on both sides. Despite their successes, the German command was disappointed with the result and much embittered by the excessive losses to their Luftwaffe strength.

The wind of change was blowing. The Allies were well advanced in their preparation for the landing in North Africa (Operation Torch) which was scheduled to take place at the end of October/beginning of November. Alerted to the danger in this sphere of operations, Reichsmarschall Göring began to withdraw squadrons of his air force from bases in Norway. As a result the Allies were now able to take the initiative and switch from the defensive to the offensive.

As the year drew to its close the German High Command was beset by differences of opinion between Hitler and the commander-in-chief of the navy, Grand Admiral

Erich Raeder, and between Raeder and the commander-in-chief of the air force, Reichsmarschall Hermann Göring. Raeder had been obstinate in his opposition to many of Hitler's plans, and although Hitler recognized that the admiral was a man of skill and ability he decided that the time was not far distant when Raeder would have to go. Attacks on the Russian convoys had not brought the success he had hoped for. War materials were still reaching Murmansk and Archangel, feeding and sustaining Russian resistance along the 1500-mile front line stretching from the Barents Sea to the Black Sea. And after the early loss in the war of two of his finest battleships, *Graf Spee* and *Bismark*, the German fleet's tactical operations were inhibited by the Führer's insistence that caution be observed at all times even against an enemy force of equal strength.

There was another factor – the shortage of oil. One of Hitler's principal objectives in his Russian campaign was the acquisition of the Caucasian oilfields to feed his great war machine. In the winter battle before Moscow the Russians' stubborn resistance destroyed these hopes and the Romanian oilfields became his only source of supply. The extended lines of communication into the USSR demanded much more fuel than even this source could provide. Rationing fell most heavily on the navy as precedence had to be given to tanks and aircraft, and from this time onward naval engagements were restricted by the necessity to balance the chances of a successful outcome against the expenditure of fuel. But by December 1942 Raeder had become impatient at the German fleet's inaction and repeated his assertion that a strong surface strike against the convoys in December would be justified by the results that could be obtained.

Reluctantly Hitler agreed. Drawing on a plan he had already formulated, Raeder proposed a combined strike against the next convoy using the heavy cruiser *Hipper* and the pocket battleship *Lutzow* with destroyer escort.

In the British camp the Admiralty made plans to sail a convoy of thirty ships with a strong escort during that month. Admiral Sir John Tovey argued against the plan, pointing out that convoys could too easily be scattered over a wide area by the extreme weather conditions, making them more vulnerable to U-boat attacks. They would therefore require a larger escort screen. After lengthy discussions it was agreed that the convoy should sail in two parts, each being escorted by seven destroyers and a few minesweepers and rescue trawlers.

On 15 December the first section of sixteen ships, with the new code JW51A and with a destroyer escort, sailed for Murmansk with close cover provided by the cruisers *Sheffield* and *Jamaica* and two destroyers, with Rear-Admiral R. L. Burnett flying his flag in *Sheffield*. Admiral Tovey in *King George* V, with the 8-inch gun cruiser *Berwick* and three destroyers, provided distant cover. With *Sheffield* and *Jamaica* forming a screen well to the south, the convoy arrived in the Kola inlet on 24 December after a quiet and uneventful voyage.

The second part of the convoy, JW51B, comprising fourteen ships, set sail from Iceland on 22 December. The escort was six fleet destroyers, *Onslow*, commanded by Captain R. Sherbrooke, senior officer of the escort force, *Orwell*, *Obedient*, *Obdurate*, *Oribi* and *Achates*, the corvettes *Hyderabad* and *Rhododendron*, the minesweeper *Bramble* and two trawlers. Providing distant cover was the battleship *Anson* with Vice-Admiral Sir Bruce Fraser aboard, the 8-inch gun cruiser *Cumberland* and three destroyers. In the meantime Admiral Burnett's cruisers *Jamaica* and *Sheffield* sailed with two destroyers from the Kola inlet to rendezvous with the advancing convoy.

When the 6-knot JW51B was mid-way between Jan Mayen Island and Bear Island on 27 December it was hit by an Arctic gale of such severity that the weather became a greater threat than the enemy, separating the port wing column of five ships and at the same time delaying Burnett's cruisers. The sea rose very quickly, with mountains of water pouring over the ships. The spray, which swept almost continuously across the decks, froze where it fell, turning guard rails into twisted and grotesque ice-sculptures and masts into improbable Christmas trees. On the bridge binoculars became useless as moisture froze on the lenses. Below decks water poured down open shafts and companionways, flooding the mess decks and saturating clothing and hammocks.

In these appalling conditions it was little wonder that ships got separated from the main convoy, and their dispersal at such an early stage in the convoy's eastward haul was a matter of deep concern to Sherbrooke. At this time of the year the southernmost edge of the Great Ice Barrier left a channel only 200 miles wide between it and north Norway where the enemy bases were established, and the main body of the convoy was now approaching the area where the enemy could easily mount an attack. Worse still, the freezing snow and wind made it almost imposible to keep the guns free from ice and operational at instant notice. All Sherbrooke could do was dispatch the little minesweeper *Bramble*, under Commander H. T. Rust, DSO, RN, to search for and round up the missing ships.

By 31 December the storm had abated, the sea became

fairly calm, but snow squalls reduced the temperature even further. Unfortunately, the day before, a German submarine, U354, sighted the convoy and reported back to Norway, describing it as comprising six to ten ships slowly heading eastward and weakly escorted. When this information was received by Admiral Raeder it appeared as a heaven-sent opportunity to justify a surface operation. An easy and comfortable victory would certainly help restore the amicable and close ties he had formerly enjoyed with the Führer. A message was at once dispatched via Admiral Theodor Krancke, the naval representative, to Hitler's headquarters in east Prussia.

It appears that when Krancke arrived to submit his report Hitler was in one of his violent rages, loudly condemning the performance of the German navy and sarcastically referring to his ships lying idle in Norwegian waters as nothing but monuments of old iron. But when Krancke produced the message from Admiral Raeder that U-boat 354 had sighted a weakly escorted convoy heading east, and that he, Raeder, approved the operational dispatch of *Hipper*, *Lutzow* and destroyers to intercept and destroy, Hitler was immediately interested and with certain reservations gave his approval. While the overall operational command was given to Flag Officer, Northern Waters, Admiral Kluber at Narvik, the tactical engagement with the enemy would be overseen by Vice-Admiral Kummetz. Hitler's stricture that caution was to be the keyword and that confrontation with a superior force was to be avoided was passed down through the chain of command to Kummetz, who duly sailed from Altenfiord on 30 December.

U-boat 354 had already given the approximate position of the convoy and indicated that it was steering east at around 7 knots. A further signal was received that two British cruisers with destroyer escort were within the vicinity of the convoy. The plan that Kummetz had worked out was simple enough and reasonably sound. His two warships would separate and descend upon the convoy from the rear. The attack would be mounted from two directions, allowing one of the ships to engage the escorts while the other could annihilate the merchant ships without fear of attack.

Meanwhile, on 27 December Admiral Burnett had left the Kola inlet and headed in the general direction of the oncoming convoy JW51B. On the evening of the 30th he steered north-west with the intention of passing astern of the convoy to meet any threat from enemy surface ships. Unfortunately, due to the intervention of the gale, JW51B was some distance from the position it was expected to be, in fact nearly forty miles south and fifty miles west of the estimated rendezvous. Instead of finding himself at the rear of the convoy, Admiral Burnett was over thirty miles north of it.

A comparison of gun-power between the German force approaching the convoy and the small British screening force showed an overwhelming superiority in favour of Admiral Kummetz. On the morning of Thursday the 31st, apart from his own ship, *Onslow*, Sherbrooke had only his four escorting destroyers, the two corvettes and an armed trawler. *Onslow* and *Achates* were each armed with four 4.7-inch guns, some of them dating back to the beginning of World War I. On the other hand the battleship *Lutzow*, the heavy cruiser *Hipper* and the six destroyers mounted a total fire-power of six 11-inch, eight 8-inch, twenty-three 5.9-inch, fifteen 5-inch and twelve 4-inch guns. *Hipper* and *Lutzow* also had 4-inch and 5-inch armour-plating against which the shells of the British destroyers would have little effect.

Hardly was Kummetz out of sight of the Norwegian coast than he received a last-minute signal from Admiral Kluber which must have dispirited him. It read:

Contrary to the operational order regarding contact against the enemy, use caution even against enemy of equal strength because it is undesirable for cruisers to take any great risks.

It revealed how deeply Hitler's fears had influenced naval command. In retrospect it can be seen that had Kummetz been allowed to carry through his plan he might well have gained a notable success. At this time of year there were only about two hours of twilight which came in the mornings and gave a visibility of between five and ten miles, and it was during this period that he planned to launch his attack. Night action would have to be avoided if at all possible, for that would be when his fleet would be most vulnerable to torpedo attacks by destroyers. Furthermore, his aim was to reach a position well astern of the convoy at dawn and then race due east with his destroyers and overhaul it, attacking from two directions in order to lure the convoy's escorts to whichever of his ships was sighted first. He therefore ordered *Hipper* and *Lutzow* to separate and to position themselves seventy miles apart by dawn, *Hipper* to the north with her six destroyers and *Lutzow* to the south.

At 07.15 on the 31st, *Hipper*, heading north-east, passed across the stern of the convoy which was some twenty miles ahead. Kummetz then ordered his destroyer *Eckholdt* to investigate the shadowy silhouettes of two ships, while *Hipper* turned towards them to reduce recognition

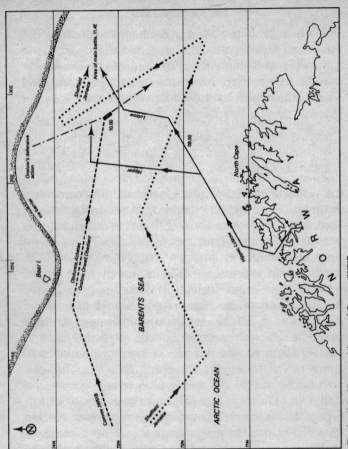

The Attack by *Hipper* and *Lutzow* of Convoy JW51B

of her own silhouette. Within the hour the situation had developed as follows. The convoy, escorted by five destroyers, two corvettes and a trawler, was approximately 200 miles north-west of the Kola inlet. Over thirty miles away to the north was Burnett with the cruisers *Jamaica* and *Sheffield*. North-east of the convoy and fifteen miles away was the minesweeper *Bramble*, still looking for the missing ships. Stealthily following on the port quarter of the merchantmen was *Hipper*, while *Lutzow* approached from starboard. The German destroyers had developed into two groups, the first comprising *Eckholdt*, *Beitzen* and Z29 shadowing the convoy, and the second comprising the *Riedel*, Z30 and Z31, each manned with four 5.9-inch guns, moving eastwards to join the oncoming *Lutzow*.

Hyderabad now sighted two destroyers to the south and they were also quickly spotted by *Obdurate*. All doubts as to their identity were dispelled when at a range of only four miles the unknown ships opened fire then turned away and disappeared. The shells fell short of *Obdurate*, and her commanding officer Captain Schlater immediately transmitted a report and fell back towards the convoy. Sherbrooke had already seen the gun flashes and ordered *Obedient*, *Orwell* and *Obdurate* to join him while heading at speed towards the rear of the convoy, its most vulnerable point. In this way he was able to gather his small force and lead it to the most advantageous defensive position.

At 09.33 Kummetz put the final part of his plan into effect, but he was now hampered by being detached from his destroyers. Although the sky was lightening, visibility was still poor and he was unable to distinguish friend from foe, for the last signal from *Eckholdt* was that she and her consorts were around the convoy. Until he was sure he dared not open fire. Moments later, however, the identity of one ship was beyond question – a British destroyer racing along between *Hipper* and the convoy, laying a thick smokescreen to hide the merchant ships. It was *Achates*, and at once *Hipper* swung to port to bring all her 8-inch guns to bear and opened fire, but although several broadsides were launched *Achates* escaped damage and continued her screening operation.

Just before *Hipper*'s attack, Sherbrooke had seen the dark silhouette of a large ship looming up through the haze on his starboard bow. He realized that his destroyers were in a most dangerous position. They had not yet had time to get into formation. *Obdurate* and *Obedient* were on the further side of the convoy and he had only *Orwell* with him. He was already aware of at least three German destroyers, each having far greater fire-power than his own ships, and now, to cap everything, the heavy cruiser with her great guns and heavily armoured hull had appeared. In theory the German force could easily have wiped out the British destroyers and then gone on to destroy the merchant fleet and their valuable cargoes. However, undaunted by the fearful odds, Sherbrooke led around to starboard, followed by *Orwell*, and closed in on *Hipper*, opening fire as they neared at a range of about five miles. At the same time *Onslow*'s torpedo tubes were made ready for firing. Torpedoes were to be her best weapon against this superior enemy, but the only chance of hitting the highly manoeuvrable cruiser would be to fire all the torpedoes at once at their greatest speed. *Hipper*'s turn to port to fire her 8-inch guns had presented Sherbrooke with a broadside-on target and, assuming that *Hipper*'s weakness lay in her fear of torpedoes, he launched a mock attack by racing in, putting the helm hard over and wheeling away, giving every appearance that a broadside of torpedoes had been fired. It was a bluff but a bluff that paid off. This was exactly the threat that Kummetz had always dreaded, and in the light of the German Naval Command's cautionary signal he broke off the engagement and ran for it, racing away from the convoy and at the same time laying down a curtain of fire from his after turrets on *Onslow*.

The retreat, albeit temporary, confirmed Sherbrooke's suspicion that the big cruiser feared a torpedo attack. It was this realization that governed his tactics for the rest of the battle. To profit from the German's fear was, however, another matter. The torpedoes were Sherbrooke's aces, and once they were fired, and should they miss, the German would know that nothing stood between him and the convoy except a few ineffectual small guns. The bluff therefore had to be exercised at every possible opportunity. By now *Obedient* had joined *Onslow* and soon *Obdurate* was seen approaching. Still with no idea of the whereabouts of the German destroyers, Sherbrooke ordered *Obedient* and *Obdurate* to return to protect the convoy while *Onslow* and *Orwell* remained to thwart any further attacks by *Hipper*. The attacks were not long in coming. Just before 10.00, Kummetz launched another thrust against the British destroyers, but was again turned away by their mock attacks. In the meantime Sherbrooke received encouraging news from HMS *Sheffield* that she and HMS *Jamaica* were racing south to give them help. Help was desperately needed, for two of *Onslow*'s four guns had frozen up. Now there were only six 4.7-inch guns against the massive fire-power of the enemy.

And what of *Lutzow*? Whether by deliberate strategy or some miscalculation, the battleship was still some thirty miles away to the south at the time *Hipper* was mounting her attacks. Soon after 10.00, *Hipper* returned and managed to fire a few ineffective salvoes at the ships in the rear of the convoy. At once *Onslow* turned towards her and opened fire with both guns at a range of nearly eight miles, scoring three hits. Futile as they may have been, it was not to Kummetz's liking and the cruiser turned away and laid a smokescreen. Five minutes later *Hipper* returned to make her fourth attack and swung round to bring all her 8-inch guns and most of her 4-inch to train on the two British destroyers. In fact while *Hipper* was firing a total of 2,200 lbs of high explosive, the best that *Onslow* and *Orwell* could offer was a mere 200 lbs. Until now the British ships had been lucky, but the frightening inequality in gun-power was too much. On top of this, *Hipper* was loading her guns with high-explosive shells that could create havoc on the thin steel plating of the destroyers and cargo ships alike, and even a near miss would scatter the ships with lethal splinters.

The cruiser's guns now began to find their range. Four shells landed in quick succession on *Onslow*, inflicting crippling damage throughout the ship and causing many casualties. The foredeck became a mass of flame, billowing up in front of the bridge and destroying the only two remaining guns. On the bridge Sherbrooke received severe wounds in the face. Covered in blood, and despite the loss of one of his eyes, he continued to direct operations. Aware that the next salvo might obliterate the ship he ordered *Onslow* to turn away, make smoke and hide in the billowing cloud.

Hipper now switched target to *Orwell*, her shells falling with alarming accuracy around the ship. At once Commander Austen fell back towards the crippled *Onslow* and made smoke to screen his leader and to cover himself. He was now faced with an agonizing decision. His was the only ship effectively positioned to fight off the *Hipper*. Should he turn to face the German cruiser and launch a torpedo atack which would probably mean the destruction of his own ship or should he continue to cover *Onslow*?

Mercifully the decision was made for him, for through the smoke and snow squalls *Hipper* was seen to turn away eastward. What made Kummetz abandon his attack at this vital moment remains a mystery, for his ship was undamaged and his fire-power vastly superior. Furthermore, he had eliminated one of the defending destroyers and his guns were finding their range to destroy the others. He would then be free to sink the convoy at leisure. But instead, with victory within his grasp, he retreated into a snow squall.

In *Onslow* the surgeon lieutenant-commander did what he could for Captain Sherbrooke in his cabin by the light of a lamp. Although in great pain, and with his left eye hanging down his cheek, Sherbrooke insisted on receiving reports of damage and continued to issue orders on the control of the ship. Eventually, however, he ordered Commander D. Kinloch, the commanding officer of *Obedient*, to take command of the flotilla and Lieutenant-Commander T. Marchand to take command of *Onslow*.

Kinloch's first order was to signal the other two

destroyers to join him. He was now left with three effective ships which were armed with only 4-inch guns. The condition of *Onslow* was critical. All her guns were out of action, she was badly on fire forward, shell splinters had punctured the engine room and boiler room, safety valves had been damaged, producing clouds of white steam amid the black smokescreen, and the ship was listing to port. Due to the volume of smoke from the forward fires, the bridge became untenable. Then came the news that one of the boiler rooms was on fire and water was flooding in. Equally serious was the discovery that most of the electric power had been cut and that radio transmission was impossible.

At 10.45 that morning, *Hipper*, with two escorting destroyers, returned to the attack and Kinloch was forced to copy the tactics that Sherbrooke had employed so successfully. With his consorts he turned towards the cruiser in a mock torpedo attack and turned away, making smoke. Seconds later *Hipper* opened fire on *Achates* which had been steaming forward and backward around the convoy providing a smokescreen. Soon she was also hit and holed forward, considerably reducing her speed, and minutes later more shells struck, one of which demolished the bridge, killing her commanding oficer Lieutenant-Commander A. Johns, with another penetrating the hull on the port side and severely damaging one of the boiler rooms. Despite the damage *Achates* managed to maintain her assignment and supplement the smokescreen between the enemy and the convoy, but her end was inevitable and at 13.00 she signalled *Northern Gem* to come alongside and take off survivors. Thirty minutes later she sank.

In the meantime *Hipper* had laid down a curtain of fire

on the three remaining destroyers, *Obedient*, *Orwell* and *Obdurate*, which persisted in darting in and firing their little 4-inch guns at the enemy. They eventually achieved their object of again turning *Hipper* away, but in so doing drove her in to the path of the minesweeper *Bramble*. The little ship never had a chance. Within seconds the eight 8-inch guns of the enemy had blown her out of the water.

But now a new crisis emerged, for the escort corvette *Rhododendron* reported a heavy ship closing in from the south. This was the *Lutzow* with her escort of three destroyers, and soon the 11-inch shells of the battleship were straddling the rear of the convoy. It was a gift of a target to Captain Stange, the commanding officer of *Lutzow*, for unlike Kummetz he could see no British destroyers to challenge him. Alarmed by the added danger, Kinloch led his destroyers round to protect the southern flank of the convoy and there laid a thick smokescreen between them and the new enemy. At the same time *Hipper* and her destroyers returned to launch another attack from four miles. Kinloch led his destroyers to the other flank to again face the cruiser, then opened fire and again adopted the mock torpedo attack used by Sherbrooke. Once more *Hipper* turned away, but in the engagement straddled *Obdurate*, her shells causing damage and casualties. Then, incredibly, *Lutzow* failed to push home her advantage, turning away from the pall of smoke and snowcloud, reporting that it was impossible to distingush between friend and foe.

What was left of the British force was now in an impossible situation. *Achates* had been sunk, *Onslow* made useless and *Obedient* and *Obdurate* badly damaged. *Orwell* remained the only ship untouched. Together, limited by their responsibility to the convoy, they faced a battleship, a heavy cruiser and six large destroyers. But help was at hand. Admiral Burnett with the cruisers *Sheffield* and *Jamaica*, approaching at their top speed of 31 knots, could now see gun flashes indicating that the British destroyers were fighting a life-or-death battle. However, Burnett could not go charging into the smoke-filled area without identifying the enemy, but by keeping to the northward on the darker horizon he hoped to pick out the enemy ships before they saw him. He was right, for as *Hipper* on her last evasive manoeuvre swung away from *Obedient* to the north, she ran straight into the gunsights of the oncoming British cruisers. In fact the German was silhouetted against the slightly lighter southern horizon and did not see *Sheffield* and *Jamaica* until they opened fire on her. She was taken completely by surprise, with her 8-inch guns trained to port, and she failed to reply until she was hit by four 6-inch shells from *Sheffield*.

For Kummetz it was now a different kind of war. He was being treated to some of his own medicine. He found himself facing the cruisers to the north while the three destroyers smokescreening the convoy separated him from *Lutzow* to the south. The great plan to annihilate JW51B, into which so much planning had gone and which on paper had seemed so easy, was now turning sour. The four shells from *Sheffield* had done considerable damage. One boiler room was flooded and out of action, reducing speed to 23 knots, and shells penetrating the port side had started fires in the hangar. In a desperate bid to avoid more damage, *Hipper* swung round in a circle to starboard and hid in the smokescreen laid by her own destroyers. *Sheffield* and *Jamaica* made chase, but then two enemy destroyers suddenly appeared out of the murk ahead of *Sheffield*'s port bow. One, the *Eckholdt*, was broadside on and in a perfect position to torpedo the British cruiser. Burnett immediately ordered *Sheffield* to steer straight towards the German, to comb a possible torpedo attack, and as she was so near he decided to ram her. At the same time, with the range coming down to point blank, he poured a pulverizing fire into the *Eckholdt* from the six guns of the two forward turrets. The German destroyer, assuming that the two big ships bearing down upon her were *Hipper* and *Lutzow*, was caught utterly off her guard. Salvo after salvo smashed into her until she was a blazing and rapidly disintegrating wreck. Such was the rapidity and intensity of the gunfire that she had no chance of using her torpedoes or even of replying from her turrets. Meanwhile *Jamaica*, slightly astern of *Sheffield*, had engaged the second destroyer, *Beitzen*, which rapidly turned away to hide in her own smokescreen.

This engagement with the German destroyer had allowed *Hipper* to escape to the west at her top speed, with the British cruisers following. Kummetz had already signalled the order for all German ships to break off the engagement and withdraw. It was a pointless exercise for Burnett to go chasing after the enemy in the dark of the Arctic night, with the convoy to the east so weakly protected. It might be argued that Burnett could have maintained his pursuit of *Hipper* and *Lutzow*, but his primary duty was the protection of the merchant ships as there was always the possibility that other enemy ships could be preparing an attack. As it was, Kummetz's forces had had enough. He should have had things all his own way, but Sherbrooke with his few destroyers had bluffed him from start to finish and sent him off smarting. While Sherbrooke's forces had suffered casualties, they had fought a courageous and gallant action against a vastly superior enemy force and had saved the convoy from utter destrucion. Just as Commander Richmond had demonstrated in *Bulldog* in defence of convoy QP11 in May, attack had once again proved the best form of defence.

The outcome of the engagement was admirably summed up by Admiral Tovey in his report:

> That an enemy force of at least one pocket battleship, one heavy cruiser and six destroyers with all the advantage of surprise and concentration, should be held off for four hours by five destroyers, and driven from the field by two 6 inch cruisers without any loss to the convoy is most creditable and satisfactory.

Although the British force had lost a destroyer and a minesweeper, the Germans had also lost a destroyer and such was the damage inflicted on *Hipper* that she was never again employed in an operational capacity. In fairness, however, the German offensive operation had been severely hampered. Whereas throughout the engagement the British destroyers' principal concern was the safety of the convoy, the German ships were restrained by the order to avoid damage to themselves. Their lamentable performance was a sharp reminder to German Naval Command that whenever their commanding officers were bound by such restrictions as those issued by the Führer victory would be impossible.

In the German camp the outcome of the engagement

was to have extraordinary repercussions. While Kummetz was leading his disconsolate force back to Norway, friction was mounting at Hitler's headquarters. A radio message from a British source had been intercepted, claiming that a large German cruiser had been damaged and a destroyer sunk. Hitler, who had been hoping for a substantial New Year's Day victory, was beside himself with rage, especially as he had not been informed of the result by either Kummetz or Raeder before the British transmission. When Raeder and Hitler eventually met, the latter, in one of his usual furies, exploded. The fleet was an utter failure, he ranted, it was a waste of resources, and it had had its last chance. All the heavy ships would be withdrawn from the Arctic and put to better use in land defence. Raeder put up a formidable defence to save his navy but it was useless. The Führer was adamant. Raeder tendered his resignation and it was accepted. To succeed him Hitler selected Admiral Karl Donitz.

On the morning of 1 January 1943 the destroyer *Onslow*, with a list of 14° and down by the bows, arrived in Murmansk where Sherbrooke, badly wounded, was transferred to hospital. It was during his stay in hospital he was told that the king had awarded him the Victoria Cross. In response to the overwhelming congratulations from the officers and men of his destroyer flotilla he dispatched the following signal:

This award is a tribute to the force in general and I hope will be taken by the next of kin of those who lost their lives, as some measure of their country's appreciation.

Some days later the following announcement appeared in the *London Gazette*.

The King has been graciously pleased to approve the award of the Victoria Cross, for valour in the defence of a convoy, to Captain Robert St Vincent Sherbrooke, DSO, Royal Navy. Captain Sherbrooke, in HMS Onslow, was the Senior Officer in command of the destroyers escorting an important convoy bound for North Russia. On the morning of the 31st December off the North Cape, he made contact with a greatly superior enemy force which was attempting to destroy the convoy. Captain Sherbrooke led his destroyers into the attack and closed with the enemy. Four times the enemy tried to attack the convoy but was forced each time to withdraw behind a smoke screen to avoid the threat of torpedoes, and each time Captain Sherbrooke pursued him and drove him outside the gun range of the convoy and towards our covering forces. These engagements lasted some hours but after the first forty minutes, HMS Onslow was hit and Captain Sherbrooke was seriously wounded in the face and lost the use of one eye. Nevertheless, he continued to direct the ships under his command until further hits on his own ship compelled him to disengage but not until he was satisfied that the next Senior Officer had assumed control. It was only then that he agreed to leave the bridge for medical attention, and until the convoy was out of danger he insisted on receiving reports of the action. His courage, his fortitude and cool prompt decisions inspired all around him. By his leadership and example the convoy was saved

from damage and was brought safely to its
destination.

The Barents Sea setback was not the only reason for the
Führer's frustration and raging temper. On the Russian
front the German position had seriously deteriorated.
The winter of 1942–3 was closing in and General von
Paulus's Sixth Army of some 250,000 men had failed to
capture Stalingrad and was now encamped outside, with
long and tenuous lines of communication and supply.
Worse still, his army was exhausted, with its flanks
thinly protected by allies of uncertain loyalties and
quality. The advice from the generals was that they
should withdraw and regroup before the Russians
mounted their winter offensive, but Hitler refused to
listen. Despite von Paulus's pleas to be allowed to retreat
while there was still time, the Führer instead demanded
that he should stand and hold his ground.

In late November 1942, in no small part thanks to the
massive supplies of tanks, planes, guns and ammunition
provided by the Allies in the northern convoys, the
Russians advanced on two fronts in an encircling assault
and trapped the German Sixth Army between the Don
and the Volga. In mid December General Manstein made
a supreme effort to break through the Russian lines in a
bid to relieve the beleagured garrison, but he failed and
had to make a hasty withdrawal which spread to all the
German southern front. Efforts to supply von Paulus's
army from the air led to crippling losses in aircraft, and
few supplies got through. The bitter cold took its toll of
hundreds of men; food and ammunition were scarce,
and worse, typhus became rampant.

On 22 January 1943 the Russians launched a massive offensive and the Sixth Army was forced back until they were pinned down in a rectangular area only eight miles long and four miles wide. Thousands were killed in the intensive artillery bombardment and air attack that followed. Finally, on 31 January, von Paulus and his staff were captured along with only 90,000 other prisoners out of a total of a quarter of a million men. The disaster destroyed Hitler's dreams of conquering Russia by sheer weight of highly trained armies, and Manstein was forced into retreat all along the southern front including the Caucasus. As the Russian winter offensive grew in strength and the bitter snowstorms intensified, so the German armies were forced from an offensive to a defensive posture. The writing was on the wall, and history about to repeat the events of Napoleon's disastrous retreat in 1812.

Grand Admiral Carl Donitz was of a different calibre to his predecessor. His determination and resoluteness appealed to Hitler, who accepted his advice far more readily than that of Admiral Raeder. Donitz had done extremely well in his ruthless campaign as head of the U-boat command, but his new post as commander-in-chief of the German navy carried little power following Hitler's decree that all the heavy ships would be withdrawn. Although initially he had agreed with Hitler on this point, he came to the same conclusion as Admiral Raeder when he carefully considered the options. In the meantime Hitler's vow, voiced in a fit of temper, had not been carried out. So, in February 1943, with some boldness it must be said, Donitz approached Hitler with a plan to use the heavy surface ships in a determined bid to halt the Arctic convoys. His intention was to bring the 43,000 ton battleship *Tirpitz*, the 32,000 ton battlecruiser *Scharnhorst*, the 12,000 ton pocket battleship *Lutzow* and a flotilla of destroyers to Altenfiord near North Cape in readiness to intercept the east-bound convoys when the opportunity arose. Against his better judgement Hitler reluctantly agreed, and by 8 March the heavy ships were in position.

Meanwhile, during January and February convoy JW52 of fourteen ships and JW53 of twenty-eight ships had sailed and reached Murmansk with the loss of only four vessels. The winter darkness provided the most favourable conditions for the convoys, and despite the fact that the Russians renewed their protests that more convoys should have been sailed the Admiralty had every reason to feel satisfied that so few ships had been lost.

It was during this period that Admiral Donitz sought a clarification from Hitler as to his responsibilities. Determined to avoid a repetition of the *Hipper–Lutzow* fiasco, he wanted a clear mandate that he alone would have the responsibility for giving the executive order to launch an attack on the British convoys when the opportunity presented itself. And in view of Hitler's record of imposing last-minute restrictions on flag officers, preventing decisive results, he furthermore needed an assurance that once he sailed he would not be restrained by special instructions from a higher authority. Such was the unpredictability of Hitler's moods that he approved, albeit begrudgingly, his admiral's conditions.

When intelligence reports reached Admiral Tovey of the concentration of powerful German ships at Altenfiord, which were obviously waiting to pounce on any eastward-moving convoy, he raised the utmost objections to sailings during the perpetual daylight of the summer period. He considered that the only response to this threat would be to sail the British battle fleet to oppose it, but that unless a strong carrier force could be provided such a move would be the height of folly. Finally the Admiralty agreed, and on 30 March Churchill reluctantly had to advise Stalin of the decision and the reasons for it. Stalin's reply was churlish in the extreme, referring to 'this unexpected action as a catastrophic diminution of supplies of arms and military raw materials to the USSR', and he went on: 'You realize of course that the circumstances cannot fail to affect the position of the Soviet troops.' In an effort to mollify Stalin Churchill dispatched another letter, on 16 April, describing the success achieved in bombing raids on Germany and against Rommel's army in North Africa, to which he received a most warm and friendly reply.

During the summer months of 1943, while no convoys passed through the Barents Sea, the German fleet swung idly at their moorings in Altenfiord. Sea-going and target practice was suspended because of the shortage of fuel oil, and this inactivity made *Tirpitz* in particular a tempting target for a daring raid by a little-known branch of the Royal Navy. Six midget submarines known as X craft were towed by operational submarines to the mouth of the fiord and there released to find their own way through the anti-submarine nets surrounding *Tirpitz*. Two of the X craft, each carrying two charges of two tons of amatol, managed to get through, and after a hair-raising adventure all four charges were attached to the hull of the great battleship. The craft then withdrew, surfaced, and were captured and held prisoner. Minutes later the eight tons of amatol exploded. The effects were quite remarkable. The two forward turrets of 15-inch guns were made useless, the three turbine engine rooms were destroyed and a variety of other damage was inflicted which put her completely out of action for the next six months. (The fact that repairs were effected so quickly was a great credit to the efficiency and capability of the German engineers and dockyard workers.) For their outstanding heroism the leaders of the two craft, Lieutenant Place and Lieutenant Cameron, were each awarded the Victoria Cross. By this one remarkable and memorable act of valour the mighty *Tirpitz* was seriously crippled, thus easing the threat to the running of convoys. The importance of this event can be measured by Churchill's statement to his chiefs of staff in January 1942 when he described how the crippling of this one ship would affect the whole strategy of the war.

CHAPTER FIFTEEN

The Destruction of the
Scharnhorst

In 1943 important changes were made in both the British and German naval commands that were to have far-reaching effects on the eventual outcome of the sea war. In May, Admiral Sir John Tovey handed over his command to Admiral Sir Bruce Fraser, a man of outstanding tactical skill, and in August the First Sea Lord, Admiral Sir Dudley Pound, also resigned his post, after suffering a stroke, and was succeeded by Sir Andrew Cunningham, who had commanded with such distinction in the Mediterranean war. On the German side, in order to improve the unwieldy chain of command connecting the German Admiralty with its fleet commander, Admiral Donitz had given instructions that movement orders would be relayed directly from the Commander-in-Chief, Northern Group, Admiral Schniewind to Vice-Admiral Kummetz, flag officer commanding the battle group at Altenfiord.

By late spring, with such stirring events taking place on the Russian front, it was clear to most that the turning point had been reached. All the ground that the German armies had gained in 1942 had been lost and they were now 250 miles from Moscow and still being driven westward. They had suffered incredible losses in men and war materials and were now inferior to the Russians in battle. There was also good news on other fronts. The British and American air forces had gained the initiative and were raining thousands of tons of bombs on German factories and cities, and in North Africa all resistance from Rommel's so-called invincible army had ceased, following heavy casualties and the capture of a quarter of a million prisoners.

The tide had turned in favour of the Allies, and as the end of war came in sight it became necessary for the Allied leaders to formulate conditions for peace when the time arrived. On 30 June 1943, at the Guildhall in London, Churchill issued the following statement:

We, the United Nations, demand from the Nazi, Fascist, and Japanese tyrannies unconditional surrender. By this we mean that their will-power to resist must be completely broken, and that they must yield themselves absolutely to our justice and mercy. It also means that we must take all those far-sighted measures which are necessary to prevent the world from being again convulsed, wrecked and blackened by their calculated plots and ferocious aggressions. It does not mean, and it never can mean, that we are to stain our victorious arms by inhumanity or by mere lust of vengeance, or that we do not plan a world in which all branches of the human family may look forward to what the American Declaration of Independence finely calls 'life, liberty, and the pursuit of happiness'.

This was later followed by a deposition from the president of the United States:

The United Nations have no intention to enslave the German people. We wish them to have a normal chance to develop in peace, as useful and respectable members of the European family. But we most certainly emphasize the word 'respectable' for we intend to rid them once and for all of Nazism and Prussian militarism and the fantastic and disastrous notion that they constitute the 'Master Race'.

Unconditional surrender was the keyword.

On 15 November the first of the new winter convoys, JW54A, set out for Murmansk; followed a week later by JW54B. Both arrived unmolested. The next convoy, JW55A, comprising nineteen ships and supported by Admiral Fraser's flagship *Duke of York*, sailed on 12 December and also suffered no interference. Meanwhile, British Intelligence had learned that the Germans had become aware of convoy movement, and Fraser rightly assumed that action by the Altenfiord battle squadron could be imminent. He was so certain that at least the *Scharnhorst* would come out to attack the next convoy that he held a number of night exercises, placing the cruiser *Jamaica* in the role of the German ship. The battlecruiser *Scharnhorst* was a warship of some reputation. Launched at Wilhelmshaven in October 1936, she had a displacement of 32,000 tons with a crew of 1800 and an armament of nine 11-inch, twelve 5.9-inch and fourteen 4-inch guns, and thirty-two smaller anti-aircraft guns.

Right from the outset of war she had a lucky career with her sister ship *Gneisenau* operating in the Atlantic. In November 1939 she sank the *P & O* liner *Rawalpindi* south-east of Iceland and in June 1940, during the evacuation of Norway, she destroyed the aircraft-carrier *Glorious* and the two destroyers *Acasta* and *Ardent* with the loss of 1500 men. Further forays into the Atlantic during 1941 brought success in the sinking of twenty-two merchant ships with a total of 116,000 tons.

When Admiral Donitz received the news that convoy movements were afoot he informed Hitler of his intention to sail *Scharnhorst* along with destroyers of the battle group to strike at the next convoy. He must have recognized that with the onset of winter there would be a change in operating conditions. British destroyers would have the advantage in the darkness of delivering torpedo attacks, and even the brief period of Arctic twilight would be barely adequate to mount a commanding raid if the convoy were well guarded. They were also favoured by the weather, since violent gales, blizzards, paralyzing cold and enormous waves reduced the ability of U-boat patrols and air reconnaissance to locate the convoy. Dontiz would also have been aware of the superiority in British radar technique which could be all-important in a night engagement. Moreover, Vice-Admiral Kummetz, commanding the battle group at Altenfiord, had just been sent on prolonged sick leave and his place had been taken by Flag Officer, Destroyers, Rear-Admiral Erich Bey. Although Bey was undoubtedly a man of courage and experience, his experience had been mainly established with the destroyer fleet, and his bluff, optimistic disposition, allied to a belief in good luck, did not mark him as one of the greatest German admirals of his time.

On 20 December convoy JW55B, comprising nineteen ships and escorted by the ten destroyers *Impulsive*, *Scourge*, *Huron*, *Orwell*, *Iroquois*, *Haida*, *Onslaught*, *Onslow*, *Whitehall* and *Wrestler*, set out for Murmansk. At the same time the returning convoy RA55A sailed from Murmansk, homeward-bound. This consisted of twenty-two empty cargo vessels escorted by the eight destroyers *Musketeer, Opportune, Virago, Matchless, Ashanti, Milne, Meteor* and *Athabascan*, as well as the 8-inch gun cruiser *Norfolk* and the 6-inch gun cruisers *Sheffield* and *Belfast*, with Rear-Admiral Burnett flying his flag in the latter.

To counter and hopefully trap the *Scharnhorst* in its expected raid on the convoy, Admiral Fraser in the battleship *Duke of York*, with the cruiser *Jamaica*, the destroyers *Savage, Scorpion* and *Saumarez* and the Norwegian destroyer *Stord*, headed northwards, keeping as close as he could to the convoy route without betraying his presence. In the meantime a German reconnaissance plane had spotted the outgoing convoy of JW55B and reported its composition, its escort, course and speed to headquarters in Norway.

By noon on 24 December the convoy was between Jan Mayen Island and Bear Island and some 400 miles north-east of Fraser's covering force. But now the weather worsened, slowing the eastward advance, a matter of grave concern to the admiral who was keenly aware that if a surface attack were to develop his force would be too far away to give the protection he had planned. Furthermore, Admiral Burnett's force covering the returning convoy was well to the east. To close the gap he took the unusual step of breaking radio silence to order the escort commander of JW55B to slow his advance for three hours while *Duke of York* and its escorting force increased speed from 15 to 19 knots.

By Christmas morning it was obvious which of the two convoys was being earmarked for attack, since RA55A had gone apparently undetected while JW55B was being shadowed by air and U-boat reconnaissance. In order to give the convoy further protection, therefore, Fraser again broke radio silence with a signal to Burnett to transfer four of his destroyers to JW55B and to divert RA55A further northward. This brought the outgoing escort's strength to fourteen destroyers, a force which if attacked by the German battleship would prove a formidable foe and the sort of opposition most likely to be feared.

Meanwhile, German radio intelligence had failed to intercept Admiral Fraser's two transmissions, and Donitz therefore had no idea that the 14-inch *Duke of York* was at sea hoping to intercept the *Scharnhorst*. In his assessment of the situation he had come to the conclusion that the eastward-bound convoy was an easy target. The area through which it would sail was within comfortable reach of Altenfiord, while the British cruisers and destroyers would be no match for the 32,000-ton battlecruiser with her nine long-range 11-inch guns.

On the morning of the 26th, Admiral Bey and his staff boarded the *Scharnhorst* and slipped out of Altenfiord with five destroyers, heading north at 25 knots. However, Dontiz's enthusiasm for the operation was somewhat moderated by Admiral Schniewind's apprehension that the weather was unfavourable and that there was too little information coming from air reconnaissance, but Schniewind's suggestion that only the destroyers should sail was swiftly dismissed. The battle group would sail as planned. The ostensible reason for the sortie was of course to prevent supplies reaching the enemy on the Russian front, but could it have been that Donitz was more concerned to establish his credibility with Hitler by snatching what he assumed would be an easy victory?

At the last minute, however, it appears that he began to have misgivings, for although Bey had been given considerable latitude in his method of attack, only a few hours after putting to sea a signal was sent from Naval Command limiting his authority. A concerted attack would only be permissible if weather conditions and visibility were favourable, and Bey was to disengage if heavy enemy forces were encountered. Was he doubting the success of the foray? For a man who had deplored Hitler's last-minute restrictive orders to his flag officers and who had himself demanded autonomy as commanding officer it seems extraordinary that Donitz should now be vacillating.

Despite the weather, *Scharnhorst* raced steadily northward through the great seas, but the accompanying destroyers wih their heavy 5.9-inch guns were rolling dangerously in the heavy swell. Fortunately for the British, Bey made his first mistake when at midnight he broke radio silence to inform Naval Group North that destroyer action would be drastically curtailed by the atrocious weather conditions. To which he received the unwelcome reply that if destroyer engagement was impossible then solo action by *Scharnhorst* might be the only alternative. This message was picked up by the British Intelligence listening service and immediately passed to *Duke of York*. In the very early hours of the morning of 26 December Fraser received the signal he had been waiting for: 'Admiralty appreciates *Scharnhorst* at sea.' His hunch had proved right.

To briefly summarize the British and German positions at this point:

1. – Admiral Fraser with his force was heading east some 200 miles south-west of the convoy to cut off *Scharnhorst*'s retreat.

2. – Vice-Admiral Burnett's cruisers were 150 miles east of convoy JW55B, heading west.

3. – Convoy RA55A, westbound, was 200 miles west of Bear Island.

4. – JW55B, eastbound, was fifty miles south of Bear Island.

5. – *Scharnhorst* 100 miles from JW55B, was steering north with her five destroyers.

Between 04.00 and 06.00 that morning Admiral Fraser twice broke radio silence, to order Burnett to report his position and secondly to direct the convoy to head north-east, which would increase *Scharnhorst*'s difficulties in finding it and improve his chances of intercepting the German's escape route back to Altenfiord. Again the Germans failed to intercept the transmission. Now that Fraser knew the exact position of his forces, and probably also that of the enemy, he was able to set the trap.

Bey, on the other hand, was in difficulty because reports he was receiving from German intelligence sources were out-dated and misleading. One of them stated that no British ships had been detected within a scope of fifty miles, but it was dated the afternoon of the previous day. Then he made his second mistake. At 07.00, acting on the assumption that he was within striking distance of the convoy, he steered south-west and ordered his destroyers to spread out ahead and investigate. This meant that not only was their striking power dissipated but they were now sailing into a head-on sea and the full force of the gale, reducing their speed to a mere 10 knots. But worse was to follow, for without informing his destroyers, at 08.20 Bey altered course to the north. This brought him on a converging course with Burnett's cruisers, with the British forces closing at 25 knots and the *Scharnhorst* at 25 knots, the range dropping rapidly. At 09.20 the cruiser *Sheffield*, at a range of six and a half miles, suddenly sighted the German battle-cruiser, and almost immediately *Belfast* fired starshells to illuminate the enemy in the Arctic twilight.

At 09.29 the Battle of North Cape began with Burnett's cruisers opening fire. Two 8-inch shells from *Norfolk* struck the battlecruiser, one destroying her forward radar and the other starting a fire on the lower deck. Taken completely by surprise, *Scharnhorst* turned rapidly away to the south-east. Her duty was not to engage in a gun duel with the British force but to sink the convoy. As soon as she had drawn ahead of the cruisers she altered course to the north to reach JW55B. Anticipating the move, Burnett placed his cruisers between the convoy and *Scharnhorst*. Bey could perhaps have stood his ground and outgunned the British cruisers, but he was now without his destroyers which were some miles to the west. Belatedly he ordered them to join him. *Duke of York* meanwhile was steadily closing the gap from the west. By 11.30 Bey had still not found the convoy and just before noon he again dissipated his force by ordering his destroyers to leave him and recommence the search for the convoy. But this meant they had to turn west and once again head into the enormous waves. Just after noon *Belfast* again picked up the *Scharnhorst* on radar fifteen miles away, and by 12.20 the cruisers were near enough to open fire at five miles. Once more she veered away to prevent the British destroyers mounting a torpedo attack. Then followed a gun duel in which *Norfolk* suffered badly. One 11-inch shell destroyed a turret, causing many casualties, and another smashed all her radar sets except one. The superior speed of the German ship was now proving effective, for the British cruisers dropped further and further astern. Determined not to lose her, Burnett applied himself to the chase.

In this second phase of the battle Bey became aware that the British force had a remarkably efficient radar system. Twice they had found him in the dark and the storm and had been able to mount an attack. In the light of his earlier instructions from Naval Command not to take unnecessary risks, he decided to call off the action and head south-east for home at 28 knots. But unwittingly he was steering on a course which would bring him straight into the guns of *Duke of York* and *Jamaica*, converging from the west.

Three hours earlier a German reconnaissance plane had reported a radar contact to the Luftwaffe Group, Lofoten, of several small ships and one large to the west (this was the *Duke of York* group), but it was not until just after 13.00 that Bey received the report and even then it omitted reference to the one large ship. If he had known it was a battleship force approaching he could have plotted the probable interception point and acted accordingly, but in the event he held fixedly on to his course for Altenfiord and home.

Meanwhile, his destroyers were still slogging west into the teeth of the gale, searching for the convoy, and at about 13.00 they passed within nine miles of it without spotting anything. An hour later Bey ordered them to break off. The flotilla leader, Captain Johannsen, immediately queried the signal, uncertain whether it related to the attack on the convoy or to the whole operation.

Minutes later came the signal 'Return to base'. It was an order that Bey was to bitterly regret.

During the afternoon, Burnett, with *Sheffield*, *Norfolk*, *Belfast* and their four accompanying destroyers, continued to trail the *Scharnhorst* while maintaining communication with *Duke of York*. *Scharnhorst* was now slipping into the trap Fraser had rehearsed with *Jamaica*. At 16.17 the *Duke of York*'s radar picked up *Scharnhorst* at a range of twenty-two miles while the German was still unaware of the battleship's presence. By 16.32 the range was fourteen miles. Thirteen minutes later she swung to starboard to bring her turrets to bear, and simultaneously with *Belfast* fired starshells to illuminate the battlecruiser. As the shower of lights lit up the area it could be seen that *Scharnhorst* still had her guns trained fore and aft, clear proof that she had no idea of the British battleship closing in on her beam.

The last phase of the Battle of North Cape had begun. Seconds later the ten 14-inch guns of *Duke of York* and the twelve 6-inch guns of *Jamaica* thundered out and inflicted severe damage on the enemy ship. Bey immediately turned his ship to port but, harassed by fire from *Nofolk* and *Belfast* on his left flank, he was obliged to turn to starboard again. Recovering from the initial shock, *Scharnhorst* retaliated with shelling which became uncomfortably accurate for the British ships. The battle now developed into a running fight, with *Scharnhorst* constantly turning to fire broadsides at her pursuers. Almost imperceptibly the German ship began to outpace the British forces and for a while there seemed a chance that she might well shake off her pursuers. During the duel both of *Duke of York*'s masts were hit by shells which most fortunately did not explode, but one disconnected

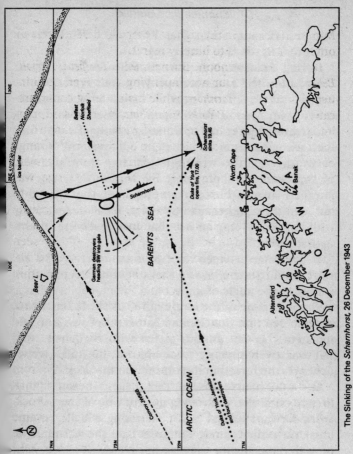

The Sinking of the *Scharnhorst*, 26 December 1943

the gunnery radar aerial. The result was a blank screen and the loss of the 'tracer eye' on which so much depended. In an attempt to repair it Lieutenant H. Bates, RNVR, from the radar section, went out on deck and climbed the ice-coated steel mainmast in the dark. It must have been a frightening experience and one demanding great courage. Clinging grimly on, with the mast swinging from left to right out over the boiling waves, the gale threatening to tear him from his hold, the ship rearing and plunging, and with shells screaming past, he managed to reach the broken ends of the cable and hold them together to bring the radar screens back to life again. It was an act that was deserving of the highest praise.

As the range between the two forces increased so the trajectory of *Duke of York*'s shells became steeper, thus increasing the angle of impact and the probability that a shell could penetrate the armoured deck. It has to be remembered that the German battlecruiser was a tough opponent, heavily armour-plated with hardened steel that was twelve inches thick around the hull, twelve inches on the turrets and six inches on the deck.

At 18.00 hours *Duke of York*'s shells began falling directly on target, destroying at least one of the *Scharnhorst*'s forward turrets and penetrating a boiler room, wreaking terrible damage. Minutes later she was hit near the waterline, greatly reducing her speed.

Bey now dispatched a signal to German Naval Command – 'We shall fight to the last shell.' At this point the destroyers *Savage*, *Saumarez*, *Scorpion* and *Stord* moved in on the port and starboard quarters, closing to 3000 yards and coming under heavy fire from the enemy. In this attack five torpedoes tore into the hull of *Scharnhorst*. By

19.00 *Duke of York* and *Jamaica* had closed the range to five miles and were scoring repeated hits, causing fires and heavy explosions. Soon the German battle cruiser ceased to make adequate reply. Torn apart by a merciless onslaught of shells and torpedoes she was reduced to a floating wreck, though she fought bravely on with her secondary armament. At 19.20 *Jamaica* and *Belfast* each fired three torpedoes. By now *Scharnhorst* was listing so heavily that none of her guns could bear on her attackers, and at 19.45 after an enormous explosion, she slipped forward by the bows, rolled over and disappeared. Out of the total complement of 2000 officers and ratings, only thirty-six survived and were picked up by the British ships.

Considering the limitations under which Bey sailed, the absence of correct information and his unfortunate error in dispersing his destroyers, the *Scharnhorst* may have been doomed from the start. None the less, the British admirals, by brilliant anticipation and efficient teamwork between battleship, cruisers and destroyers, fought and won a decisive victory.

It was the last time that a classic surface engagement in the style of the World War I Battle of Jutland was fought between battleships without the participation of fighter aircraft.

It was not until 2 January 1944, a week later, that Donitz was summoned to Hitler's headquarters to explain the loss of *Scharnhorst*. It will be remembered that it was on Donitz's recommendation that Hitler had agreed that *Scharnhorst* could sail if and when the opportunity arose, though he did so reluctantly, saying, 'You will be forced to return and admit that I was right.' The meeting must have been a very humiliating experience for the admiral. The loss of one of their few remaining operational warships was a severe blow not only to their naval strength but also to their prestige. It came at a bad time too, for the Germans were suffering one defeat after another on several fronts. In Italy they had fallen back under pressure from the invasion forces, the Normandy invasion by the Allies was imminent, and on the Russian front the Soviet armies had pushed back their invaders to the borders of Poland and Romania. Steps were taken to increase the number of U-boats in the Barents Sea, but this was a desperate move. With *Scharnhorst* sunk and *Tirpitz* damaged, the threat to the convoys was now so greatly reduced that they no longer required a battleship force to provide distant cover.

CHAPTER SIXTEEN

The Beginning of the End

The first convoy of the New Year, JW56A, sailed on 12 January 1944. It consisted of twenty ships escorted by eleven destroyers and corvettes. Three days later, in one of the many intense Arctic storms, it was attacked by U-boats. Three ships were sunk and a destroyer was damaged by a torpedo. The attack was mainly as a result of information obtained by a German agent planted in Iceland. From it the enemy was able to concentrate their U-boats across the passage of the convoy.

Although Donitz must have realized that the collapse of the Third Reich was inevitable, he had no intention of relaxing his attacks on the Russian convoys. To this end the maintenance of a powerful screen of U-boats across the path of eastward-bound British and American ships was of the utmost importance, and he set about organizing an even stronger force of submarines to achieve the success that had in the past eluded him.

Intelligence of this soon reached the Admiralty, and on 20 February 1944 a convoy of forty-two merchant ships, JW57, sailed with one of the strongest escorts of any convoy. It consisted of seventeen destroyers, one tanker, four cruisers and the escort carrier *Chaser*, with Vice-Admiral Glennie carrying his flag in the cruiser *Black Prince*. To counter them the Germans established a line of no less than fourteen U-boats in the path of the convoy, but such were the tactics of the escort and the carrier that the submarines had no chance to break through to mount an attack. Frustrated, they turned on the destroyers, torpedoing *Mahratta*. Tragically, out of the crew of about 200 only seventeen were saved. Exacting revenge, the escorts and aircraft sank two U-boats, and further losses were inflicted on the enemy when *Chaser* sank another three U-boats which were attempting to close in on the convoy.

Even greater success attended the next convoy, JW58, which left Iceland on 27 March. This big convoy comprised forty-nine merchant ships. In command of the operation was Vice-Admiral F. Dalrymple-Hamilton, carrying his flag in the cruiser *Diadem*. The close escort comprised the two carriers *Activity* and *Tracker* with thirty operational aircraft, twenty destroyers, five sloops and four corvettes. Despite the attendance of several shadowing aircraft and attacks from sixteen U-boats, aircraft sorties from the two carriers and a dogged pursuit by destroyers dispatched six enemy reconnaissance planes and four U-boats without loss to the convoy. While German Naval Command were licking their wounds, intelligence reports reached the Admiralty from a British agent at Altenfiord. He had secretly observed the work being carried out on the damaged *Tirpitz* and was able to transmit a message to the effect that the great battleship was sufficiently repaired to allow her to go to sea. On receipt of this disturbing news the Admiralty decided that another attempt must be made to disable or sink her.

In mid April, aircraft from the home fleet carriers *Victorious* and *Furious*, supported by the Royal Air Force based in north Russia, attacked *Tirpitz* with heavy bombs.

She was hit by fourteen bombs, causing serious structural damage and killing over a hundred of her crew, and was subsequently moved further south to Tromso Fiord, a move that was most agreeable to the British for it brought her two hundred miles nearer to Britain and within range of home-based heavy bombers. Nevertheless, such was the skill and efficiency of the German engineers and dockyard repair labour force that the threat of *Tirpitz* still loomed over the Barents Sea, and another attempt to immobilize the ship was made by Admiral Sir Henry Moore with his carrier force. Although his planes reached the target successfully, warning of the British raid alerted the German defence units in time for them to set up a smokescreen which hid the battleship completely.

By now the Kola inlet was cluttered with many empty merchant ships waiting for escort. On 28 April the homeward-bound convoy RA59 of forty-five ships sailed for Iceland with an escort of sixteen destroyers and the carriers *Activity* and *Fencer* under the command of Rear-Admiral R. McGrigor, flying his flag in the cruiser *Diadem*. On this voyage one merchant ship was lost while the escort carriers' planes sank three U-boats.

In June came the news the world had been waiting for when the Second Front opened with the invasion of Normandy. This at last brought relief to the Soviet Union which, despite the successes on the Eastern Front, was still paying dearly in men and materials; by the end of hostilities the Russians would have lost a total of twenty million men.

The success of the Allied escort carrier aircraft against U-boats had proved so effective that the Admiralty were encouraged to prepare the next convoy, JW59. On 15

August thirty-three ships sailed with a heavy escort consisting of the cruiser *Jamaica* and eighteen destroyers, frigates and corvettes and commanded by Vice-Admiral F. Dalrymple-Hamilton in the carrier *Vindex*. Despite the heavy escort one U-boat succeeded in penetrating the defence screen, torpedoing the sloop *Kite* with the loss of 190 men. On this voyage and that of the returning convoy RA59, due retribution was exacted by the sinking of four U-boats.

In July, Sir Bruce Fraser had been succeeded by Admiral Sir Henry Moore as commander-in-chief of the home fleet, and one of Moore's first priorities was the further immobilization of the *Tirpitz*. During August he mounted three more attacks on the German battleship, but such was the effectiveness of the ship's armour-plating that although several hits were obtained no serious damaged was caused.

It was clear that bigger and better bombs were needed if the mighty battleship was to be destroyed. The mission was now placed in the charge of the Royal Air Force, and on 15 September 1944 twenty-eight Lancaster bombers, each carrying a 12,000lb blockbuster bomb, set out from their base in north Russia for Altenfiord. Once over the target the enemy's anti-aircraft guns set up a massive barrage of flak, but the Lancasters succeeded in scoring one direct hit on the fo'c'sle of the *Tirpitz* which stripped back the armour-plated deck like a piece of cardboard. As a fighting ship she was again out of action, but in order to finish her off it was decided that another attack must be launched at the first opportunity. The Germans had given up all hope of restoring her as a threat to shipping in the Barents Sea, and Admiral Donitz, aware that she could only be used as a floating gun ship in the defence of Norway should the British attempt to invade, gave instructions that she be moved to another anchorage near Tromso. This was accomplished towards the end of October.

On 12 November twenty-eight Lancasters, each carrying a blockbuster, launched another raid. Except for intense anti-aircraft fire the run-in over the target was without opposition, and they immediately set about the destruction of the ship that had posed such a threat to the home fleet and to the lifeline of supplies to the Soviet Union. Most of the 12,000 lb bombs were on target, hitting the battleship dead amidships and aft, penetrating deep into the hull. Several other near misses blew gaping holes in her side. Following one enormous explosion the 43,000 ton *Tirpitz* capsized with the tip of her masts resting on the bottom. Her massive armour-plating of 12.6 inches of hardened steel along the main belt, 14 inches around the turrets and an 8-inch deck plating was no match for the 150 tons of high explosives that rained down upon her. Of her 1800 crew, 1000 were killed. It was an ignominious end to the pride of the German navy, a mighty ship which had never fired a gun in anger.

After the destruction of *Tirpitz* the remaining major surface units were withdrawn from the Russian convoy routes. The cruisers *Prinz Eugen* and *Hipper*, the light cruisers *Nürnberg* and *Leipzig* and the two pocket battleships *Lutzow* and *Admiral Scheer* were sent to the Baltic, where until the end of hostilities they were employed in bombarding land targets and in the evacuation of retreating troops and wounded. But during the autumn and winter of 1944–5 German Naval Command pressed on with their efforts to attack convoy shipping in spite of the fact that defeat was inevitable. There were only seven more eastward-bound convoys before the war ended, and during these voyages three more U-boats and seventeen aircraft were destroyed.

In Europe the tide of victory surged on relentlessly, with the Soviet armies advancing from the east and the British and Americans from the west. The end of the Third Reich was rapidly approaching, and by the spring of 1945 the German position was utterly hopeless. However, the exhilaration of the Allies' pending victory was bated by the news of President Roosevelt's sudden death on 12 April at Warm Springs in Georgia, USA. The news came as a great blow, particularly to Churchill, who 'was overpowered by a sense of deep and irreparable loss'. In a letter to Harry Hopkins, the personal confidant of the American president, he wrote:

> I feel with you that we have lost one of our greatest friends and one of the most valiant champions of the causes for which we fight. I feel a very painful personal loss, quite apart from the ties of public action which bound us so closely together. I had a true affection for Franklin.

As Churchill later said, 'Roosevelt died at the supreme climax of the war, and at the moment when his authority was most needed to guide the policy of the United States.' The new president, Harry Truman, was now faced with the responsibility of conducting America's part in the final stages of World War II.

On 25 April, with time running out, Heinrich Himmler, head of the dreaded Gestapo, knowing that the German civilian population would receive little mercy from the Russians after the way millions of Soviet citizens had been butchered and annihilated, tried to negotiate a separate peace with the Western Allies. It was a cunning move to try to sow discord between the Allies and Russia. Unimpressed, Churchill immediately informed Stalin of the situation:

> There can be no question, as far as His Majesty's Government is concerned, of anything less than unconditional surrender simultaneously to the three major powers ... until this happens, the attack of the Allies upon them on all sides and in all theatres where resistance continues will be prosecuted with the utmost vigour.

Stalin replied:

> I consider your proposals ... for unconditional surrender on all fronts, including the Soviet front, the only correct one. Knowing you, I had no doubt that you would act in this way.

The demand for unconditional surrender was conveyed to Himmler, and when he was eventually arrested, on 21 May, rather than face trial for his brutal and heinous crimes against humanity, he bit open a phial of cyanide hidden in his mouth and died instantly.

By 25 April the Soviet armies were on the outskirts of Berlin, engaged in bitter street-fighting with the few fanatical Nazis who had not fled westward to surrender to the advancing Allies. The Russian and Allied armies had cut Germany in two. The Nazi empire was doomed and Adolf Hitler was about to perish. The end of the dictator came on 30 April when, hiding in a concrete bunker in Berlin with a few of his immediate staff, and with the ever-nearing bombardment of heavy guns ringing in their ears, he concluded his final arrangements. At 3.30 that afternoon he shot himself in the mouth. At his side lay Eva Braun whom he had secretly married in the last few hours. She, like Himmler, had taken poison. According to Hitler's last wishes, their bodies were taken into the courtyard, petrol poured over them and burnt. Outside, as the bombs and shells demolished the centre of the city, the so-called glorious Third Reich was reduced to nothing more than a pile of dust. That same day a telegram reached Admiral Donitz informing him that the Führer had appointed him as his successor.

Everywhere the Axis powers were in full retreat. In Italy, on 2 May, over a million troops laid down their arms, and on 4 May General Montgomery accepted the surrender of over 2,500,000 Germans in Europe. On 7 May the instrument of total and unconditional surrender was signed and on 9 May it was formally ratified.

The Allied successes on land have tended to obscure the many impressive victories at sea. There can be no doubt that the enormous weight of war material sent across the Barents Sea by America and Britain, especially in the early period of the war, played no small part in assisting the Soviet Union to defeat the Germans. In the earlier convoys, losses in ships and men were heavy, but later, as the number and efficiency of escorts increased, Allied losses diminished and Germany's mounted. Altogether over 900 U-boats were destroyed in the Arctic and Atlantic while Germany's surface fleet suffered utter defeat. The big ships, which in the last few months of the war had been active in the Baltic, were either sunk or severely crippled. At Gdynia the battlecruiser *Gneisenau* was just a hulk when it fell into Russian hands, at

Wilhelmshaven American bombers sank the cruiser *Köln*, two old battleships were scuttled and British bombers sank the *Scheer* and the *Lutzow*. When the British entered Kiel they found nearly every building destroyed and the cruisers *Hipper* and *Emden* derelict, heavily damaged by bombs. The only vessels of any size still afloat were the *Prinz Eugen*, the *Nürnberg* and the *Leipzig* lying in Danish ports.

These ships and about fifteen destroyers and some torpedo boats were all that remained of the German fleet. Only the U-boats and a few smaller craft fought to the end. When Donitz issued the order to his U-boats to surrender following the formal ending of hostilities, there were nearly fifty still active at sea which eventually surrendered. Over one hundred others gave themselves up in harbour, while a further two hundred, defiant to the last, were either scuttled or destroyed by their own crews.

The cost to the Allies of maintaining the supply of war equipment to Murmansk and Archangel had been heavy. Over one hundred merchant ships and nineteen war-ships including two cruisers had been lost, resulting in the deaths of nearly 900 merchant sailors and nearly 2000 officers and men of the Royal Navy. But the United States and Britain had honoured their promise to the Soviet Union, and over the period of 1941–5 a massive total of four million tons of war equipment was escorted across the Barents Sea. The part that the men of the Royal Navy and the merchant navy played in fighting their way through the 'Gateway to Hell' is beyond praise, and the fact that their ships were not designed to cope with the incredibly harsh conditions of Arctic warfare, that they were ill-equipped in fire-power, and often outnumbered, is a tribute to the endurance and courage of the men who sailed them.

But, as Winston Churchill said in a speech to the House of Commons in May 1940: 'Victory at all costs, victory in spite of all terror, victory however long and hard the road may be; for without victory there is no survival.'

BIBLIOGRAPHY

Cajus Becker, *Hitler's Naval War* (MacDonald & Jane, 1974)

Ian Campbell, *The Kola Run* (Futura, 1975)

Brian Schofield, *The Russian Convoys* (Batsford, 1964, and Pan, 1971)

Fritz-Otto Busch, *The Sinking of the Scharnhorst* (Futura, 1974)

Harold Wheeler, *People's History of the Second World War: September 1939 to December 1940* (Odham Press)

Richard Humble, *Hitler's High Seas Fleet* (Pan/Ballantyne, 1972)

J. C. Taylor, *German Warships of World War II* (Ian Allan, 1966)

Paul Lund and Harry Ludlam, *PQ17, Convoy to Hell* (New English Library, 1973)

Winston Churchill, *The Second World War* (Cassell & Co., 1948)

INDEX

249

Index

Index

Index

253

Index

Index